INTRODUCTION
to

TOP
EXECUTIVE
MANAGEMENT

HOW TO TURN
EVERY OPPORTUNITY
INTO SUCCESS

RYUHO OKAWA
IRH Press

Contents

CHAPTER ONE

Happy Science's Management Philosophy
~ 17 Points that Form the Core of Management ~

Introduction—What Is Management?

1. Knowledge-based Management
— Aim to Become a Learning Organization

2. Time-Based Management
— Paying Attention to the Pace of Work

3. Do Not Fear Innovation

10. The Logic of "Shallow, Wide and Long"

11. Using Your Own Capital
— Concept of "Dam Management"

12. Top-Down Paradigm

13. Personnel Policies Based on the Merit System
— Giving Second Chances

14. The Theory of Decentralization

15. Theory of Eliminating Strata

16. Theory of Restructuring
— Boldly Dispose of Your Work

17. Steadiness and Boldness [Conclusion]

CHAPTER TWO

Management Tips:
The Wisdom to Survive Deflation

1. The Correct Way of Looking at Deflation

2. Prosperity during Deflation

Q&A Session

↶ CHAPTER THREE ↷

Introduction to Top Executive Management
~ The ideals as top management ~

3. Failure Is the Best Teacher

4. Management Philosophy Brings Growth to a Company

5. The Struggle Against Limits of Ability

Q&A Session

Preface

Top executives will soon find themselves in a truly, truly difficult age. We will once again see an age of turbulence. I am always hoping that the efforts of the individual and the heroic dispositions of entrepreneurs will blossom.

However, for the next 10 years, we will have to idly watch in sadness as many entrepreneurs endowed with enthusiasm and talent get swallowed up by the tides of the age, similar to being pulled in like little rafts in a violent whirlpool. As the public opinion chose an unfortunate future, the people will reap what they have sown[*].

The times will drag Japan into the tide of "totalitarian socialism." As the regime is aiming to bring the downfall of the nation, CEOs must keep their best weapon in good condition, every day.

Ryuho Okawa
Founder and CEO of Happy Science Group
November 2009

---

[*] In August 2009, 3 months before this book was published, the Democratic Party of Japan, who had totalitarian socialism-like tendencies, came into power for the first time after winning the general elections by a landslide.

Chapter One

Happy Science's Management Philosophy

~ 17 Points that Form
the Core of Management ~

Lecture given on September 30, 1996

Introduction— What Is Management?

Gaining results that Exceed the sum of your resources

In this chapter entitled, "Happy Science's Management Philosophy," I would like to give teachings that may be helpful to those of you who aim to become independent business people, who are currently managers at a company, and so on. Here I explain my thinking, which is a distillation of more than 20 years since the founding of Happy Science. On this occasion, I will take a generalized or introductory approach.

In 10 more years, I expect to solidify and systematize my thinking on business philosophy. In this chapter, I will present the way of thinking I have developed and used to manage Happy Science so far.

There are, of course, people who have doubts on whether or not management philosophy can be applied to a religious organization. On previous occasions, when I gave interviews with members of the mass media, there were some people who found it extremely strange for a religion to teach on business management. So, I would first like to address this point.

If the purpose of a business philosophy was solely to make money, then business philosophy will not likely connect directly with religious thinking. However, I do not believe that business should only involve the pursuit of profit. Rather, I believe that management is to use people, materials, money, information and other business resources in order to gain results that exceed the sum of their individual parts.

For example, if you have a hundred people each doing his or her own individual work separately, then the sum value of their efforts cannot exceed that of a hundred people. However, if they perform their jobs under a single management policy and with guidance from excellent leadership, they will be able to produce results that exceed the collective value of the work of a hundred people.

If there is a good leader present, better work can be produced than the total work of a hundred different people acting individually. This is quite obvious.

The same can be said about the use of materials. Rather than having individuals use materials and resources haphazardly as he or she sees fit, if you think about how to achieve greater production using the available facilities or tools, you could add value to the existing materials.

Furthermore, the same holds true for capital. Individuals may have their own funds or savings, but such money will never do work beyond earning interest from the bank. In contrast, for example, if people were to pool their funds together, collect more than a certain amount and use that money as enterprise capital, they could engage in business effectively with a big investment.

This is also true for information. Say that a taxi driver has a certain piece of information. This information is not of any particular use to the taxi driver to drive his taxi. However, should there be someone among his customers who requires that information and hears it from that taxi driver, then naturally that piece of information will create value.

The taxi driver might have heard from a previous customer that recently a certain stock had been acting in a certain way. Perhaps the taxi driver told this piece of information to another customer, a businessman who had just returned from overseas and knew nothing of that development. The businessman may be surprised to hear such news, get on his cell phone right away and transact some related business.

In this manner, a piece of information can come to have economic ramifications. So, various pieces of information that are spread out among different individuals can be accidentally picked up and give rise to real results.

Within an organization, however, people should not be relying on mere chance or serendipities. You need to create an organization where appropriate information is conveyed to

What is Management?

People Materials

Money Information

→ Results

To use business resources to gain results
that exceed the sum of their individual parts

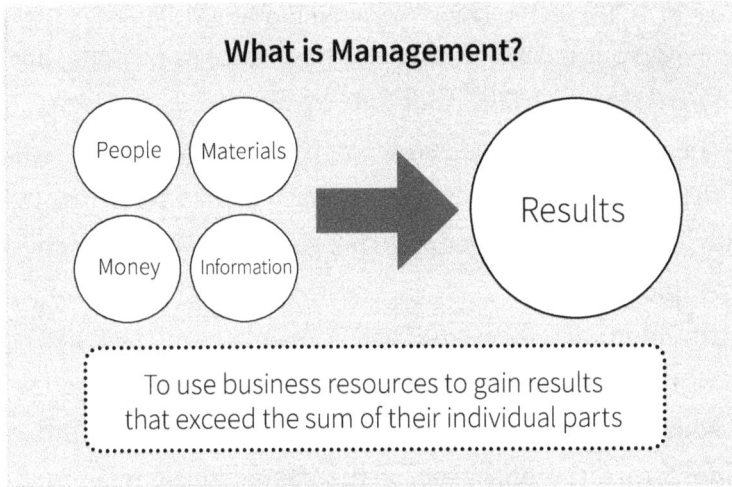

the sections or people that need it, so that proper decisions can be made and produce good results.

Management methods therefore exist in order to use people, materials, money and information to produce results that exceed the sum of these individual components. If this is done in a superior manner, management will produce impressive results and the organization will develop further.

In this way, a business started by one or two people can very well grow to a company with 50 or 100 employees, or even 1,000 or 10,000 employees. Such a transformation is truly amazing.

The approaches can vary depending on the business involved, so it is difficult to give a hard-and-fast formula, but there are always certain rules for progress.

In the modern age, even at the personal level, many of the problems we face are financial in nature. Thus, by studying the principles of progress, you can solve the worries of people today.

In addition, since quite a few people earn their living by working at companies, if the companies are tottering or going bankrupt, that constitutes a great peril. In order to normalize the operation of the company, studying such kind of management theory will not only prevent potential trouble but also promote happiness.

Management theory is included in The Principle of Progress

In the Fourfold Path taught at Happy Science, namely Love, Wisdom, Self-reflection and Progress, the Principle of Progress incorporates this kind of management philosophy or thinking. Since religions today deal with people living in social systems that did not exist in the ages of the Buddha or Jesus Christ, they should naturally discuss management theory.

When you look at religions as an organized body, they are some of the largest organizations on the face of the earth. A company may grow from being a one-man operation to one with a handful, 50, 100, or even 1,000 or 10,000 employees. In some cases, a corporation may even become a colossal organization with 100,000 or 200,000 employees. An army may be bigger than a company, but a religion has the potential to become even larger than an army. A global religion has an organization that dwarfs even an army.

That is why organizational theory for religions, in a sense, may cover the largest organizations operating in the world today.

Within a religion, large numbers of individuals share the same principles and operate in an organized manner under leaders. In addition to having a vertical stratification, a religion also has a horizontally-linked stratum. Furthermore, with a large number of individuals acting together, a religion naturally will be faced with logistical funding issues.

In that sense, I believe religions can be analyzed from a management perspective when considered solely in terms of the movements of people and money, regardless of the content of their teachings.

1

Knowledge-based Management— Aim to Become a Learning Organization

Knowledge is the most valuable business resource

Analyzing Happy Science's methodology and characteristic of management up to this point, the first thing which comes to mind is that Happy Science uses knowledge-based management.

Various things can be considered as business resources; iron ore, coal, petroleum, natural gas and so on are examples of physical resources. However, if you were to ask me what the most important resource will be now and in the future, without hesitation I would reply that it is knowledge. There can be no doubt on that score. Only knowledge will continue to increase steadily. Knowledge is an inexhaustible storehouse of new business resources.

In one sense, religion can be called the "ultimate software industry." Religion deals with information and values of a world that cannot be seen and the happiness that comes as a result of these things. As religion deals with the invisible, it can be referred to as the ultimate form of software-handling industry.

In looking at matters from a religious perspective, knowledge is an extremely critical business resource. Not only is it just for religion, but knowledge is the most valuable business resource for the contemporary and future industrial society, too. Moreover, knowledge is a resource that can expand and be recycled. In other words, new knowledge can give birth to new resources and results, which in turn gives birth to more new knowledge.

For Happy Science as well, knowledge-based management is fundamental. Our organization began in 1986 when it did not have even a single member. In just a little over a decade after that, we grew to become a large organization. Without a doubt, we are now in the top ranks of Japanese religions. If you ask what the factors behind this amazing development were, I would emphatically point to knowledge-based management.

Our organization has thoroughly sought to pursue intellectual elements. We have been researching the value-added elements of knowledge while gathering information. In addition, we are always conducting research on how to interweave both things of the past and things of the present and assessing the results.

Religions are sometimes referred to as a "traditional market," which considers it best to leave alone what is sanctified by time. While this is certainly true to some degree, by taking such stance, religions are unable to provide answers to the problems of people today.

For that reason, in the U.S., the general trend is to see a psychologist to discuss your problems, not the church. The principal reason for that is the lack of modernity in religions.

Another way in which religions lack modernity is, as I noted earlier, the fact that since economic principles were still not fully at play in the eras of Shakyamuni Buddha and Jesus Christ, their teachings did not fully address how to solve economic or financial problems.

As far as economic issues are concerned, these earlier religions tended to just teach people to abandon attachments. This is because the economic society was still insufficiently developed at the time.

Their teachings can be simply summed up in the following statements. "The rich are extravagant and proud, while the poor suffer. So, we must help the poor." "If a poor man yearns to become wealthy, he will suffer for it, so he must control his desires." Even in contemporary society, such way of thinking holds true to a considerable extent.

However, in line with modern management theory, we now know that overall wealth can be increased through skillful management. This is a key discovery made over roughly the last two centuries.

If each person is working separately, we cannot expect to see more production than the aggregate labor input. On the other hand, if all of the workers pool their knowledge and wisdom and do their own jobs well, it is possible to create wealth greater than if they had all worked separately. This is the hallmark of modern industrial society.

For example, an individual trying to produce steel from iron ore on his own would not be able to produce much; nor would he be able to turn that steel into something usable. However, if there is capital available to form a corporation, hire many workers and establish a division of labor, then large volumes of products can be produced that are markedly superior to any steel products that an individual could make on his own. The revenue from such an organized operation would be much larger, too.

In such a way, by increasing the overall level of wealth, we can also greatly increase the affluence of each individual. This is a philosophy that was not present during the eras of Shakyamuni Buddha and Jesus, but is the philosophy that has allowed modern and contemporary societies to enjoy tremendous increases in productivity.

This philosophy was born from the system whereby factories were established, products were manufactured and then distributed through domestic and overseas sales routes.

In addition, this philosophy finds its roots in the fact that large amounts of raw materials could be imported cheaply from foreign countries. It is therefore fair to say that at the base of all this lies an intellectual element.

This sort of knowledge-based management is being implemented at Happy Science. For that reason, Happy Science enjoys extremely powerful competitiveness compared to other religions. That is the reason why we have been so successful over such a short period and why other religious bodies have fallen by the wayside.

The gathering of many extremely sharp individuals must be considered another form of business resource. This, I believe, is where the potential for future growth resides.

Always be willing to learn

Moreover, *knowledge-based* does not refer solely to knowledge that you currently possess or being satisfied with your current level of intelligence. Knowledge that is used as a business resource can limitlessly expand into the future. Unless you are always willing to learn, you will fall behind in a year's time. This holds true for individuals, as it does for organizations. New things are constantly being created all around you.

The ways that Happy Science has used development

Knowledge-based Management
—Aim to Become a Learning Organization—

- Gather information
- Research the value-added elements of knowledge
- Pool workers' knowledge and wisdom and have them do their own jobs well
- Always be willing to learn

theory are imitated one after the other by other religious groups one, five or ten years later. However, in many cases they fail because there is something lacking.

As for what kinds of results are produced by the methods adopted by our group, there are areas that require individual research. But if someone looks only at the results and attempts to mimic the same methods, he or she will inevitably get different results. It may become like a Midas touch gone awry and backfire with dire consequences.

However, by basing your management on knowledge, you can open the path to a future society. Exactly the same thing holds true in the realm of religion, too. That is why I believe organizations should aim to become a learning organization.

2

Time-Based Management— Paying Attention to the Pace of Work

Reducing time expenditures

The second principle I want to look at is *time-based management*. This, too, is a critical element of Happy Science.

Time is a limited resource. Every one of us can have only twenty-four hours each day, and even if you add up all the time available to an organization, it will not exceed the number available to the total number of its constituent members.

Nevertheless, organizations or people with great development potential, without fail always concentrate on how to shorten the amount of time it takes to do something. Shortening time translates into development.

For example, it is a fact that Japan's GDP [gross domestic product] has soared since the advent of the *Shinkansen* [bullet train]. The reason is that the scope of what an individual can accomplish in a day has expanded tremendously. The nation's GDP has expanded compared to the old days when you had to take an overnight sleeper car to travel on the

Tokaido Line or when you had to get about by foot, now that the transportation time has been greatly reduced.

Methods for cutting down on time or increasing turnover are methods that can increase results.

Another example would be seasonal products. For example, if summer merchandise was only produced once during the summer, then the other seasons of the year are going to end up being unproductive blanks.

It is one way to think that summer merchandise can only be produced or sold during the summer, but in fact there are some summer goods that can also be produced during the winter. For example, you might have the impression that ice cream is something that is only to be produced during the summer, when in fact it can just as well be produced in the winter and then preserved. There are examples like this.

The same holds true for a curry rice shop. Some proprietors think that they have to prepare the curry after the customer arrives. But a curry shop that wants to enjoy high turnover no doubt needs to prepare the curry beforehand and freeze it.

If things are examined from a timesaving perspective, all kinds of changes could be made.

The process to create results involves asking questions such as "How can we go about reducing the time spent? How can we speed up the pace of work? How can we advance the schedule for achieving the next results?" If an issue is not resolved, you will not be able to deal with the next one, but by reducing the amount of time required to resolve each issue, you can more quickly address the next job.

The ultimate time-based management can be expressed in the proverb, "Each day has enough trouble of its own." [Matthew 6:34] There is also a Japanese phrase which says that you should live every day as if it were the only day in your life. In short, it is important to do everything you can during a given day.

This is a very important thing. Clinging to thoughts like, "I won't work until the time is ripe" or "Since other circumstances make it impossible, I'll skip doing it today" go against the spirit of time management.

It is important to think about what you can do to decrease the time involved. What can you possibly do to reduce the time needed to accomplish this procedure?

Decreasing the time involved simultaneously creates usable time. For instance, in going to a certain destination, whereas it might take three hours by bullet train, you could make it in just an hour by air. That in turn would free up two hours, making available two additional hours of usable time.

Make quicker decisions

Furthermore, time-based management also amounts to making quicker decisions. As an organization becomes larger, the number of strata or layers within it increase, which results in a delay in decision-making and a delay in the reception of information. How to abolish such a situation and reduce access time have become problems for any modern company. In order for a large organization to reduce access time, telephones, fax machines and other blessings of civilization must be used.

For example, as far as I could tell from what I saw during my own visits to India, Shakyamuni Buddha spent an awfully lot of time walking around in his 45 years of missionary work. Base camps of Shakyamuni Buddha's order were 200 to 300 km [120 to 190 mi] apart. So, he spent most of the year walking from one location to the next. Other than when he settled down at a hermitage during the summer rainy season, almost all of his time seems to have been spent walking.

Hearing this, we would have to say that his productivity was low.

Today, however, the roles that his walking accomplished are now performed by print, CDs or DVDs, or satellite broadcasts, which have resulted in increased productivity. In this manner, as compared to the past, even when human life spans are the same, the amount of time that can be productively employed has increased. By eliminating unnecessary things and shortening the amount of access time, it is possible to create more usable time.

Consequently, all developing modern companies and venture businesses use time-based management and think about how to increase the pace.

In the past, there were often cases where, for example, documents about which only the CEO could make a decision waited in his incoming tray for three days or a week. And what was the CEO doing all that time—playing golf!

Time-based Management

- Reduce time spent

- Increase turnover

- Do what you can during a given day ("Live today as if it were your last")

- Make quicker decisions

Now, however, it is normal for firms to grapple with the question of how to make quicker decisions. In fact, the trend now is to get rid of managerial approval all together. The day when it was necessary to get the approval of 20 or 30 company officials is long gone; the emphasis now is on making the decision as close as possible to the actual workplace.

I believe that two of the distinctive features of Happy Science are our commitment to knowledge-based management and time-based management. These two approaches work in the same way, regardless of whether they are applied to religion or some other entity. By using them, you can increase the rate of progress.

3

Do Not Fear Innovation

What is innovation?

The third key point is not to fear innovation. This too, I believe, is a major characteristic of our organization.

How should we understand *innovation*? One approach is to adopt the definition offered by people like the renowned economist Joseph Schumpeter—to create a new combination. This is one definition of innovation. So, innovation could be defined as the creation of something new through the joining of different things or matters of different nature.

On the other hand, Peter Drucker, the famous management guru, said something along the lines of the following: "Although most people tend to think that innovation consists of creating something new, that is not true. When your methods and system until now become obsolete, you have to be prepared to abandon what had been quite fruitful in the past. Here, it is not a question of getting rid of just one aspect; you have to be prepared to scrap all methods and systems that had been used up to this point. In this way, innovation actually is like systematic abandonment."

Both approaches to innovation are interesting. As far as innovation is concerned, normally we think mainly of creating new things through new combinations of things. For example, you can get water by combining hydrogen with oxygen. Although both hydrogen and oxygen are gases, when combined in the right proportion you end up with the liquid we call *water*, which is a completely new substance.

Furthermore, if you heat this water, it will vaporize into steam. When that happens, you can power turbines, trains or ships. By combining oxygen with hydrogen, these substances change into something totally different and perform new work.

In this manner, innovation is the power to create new things through new combinations. In addition, innovation

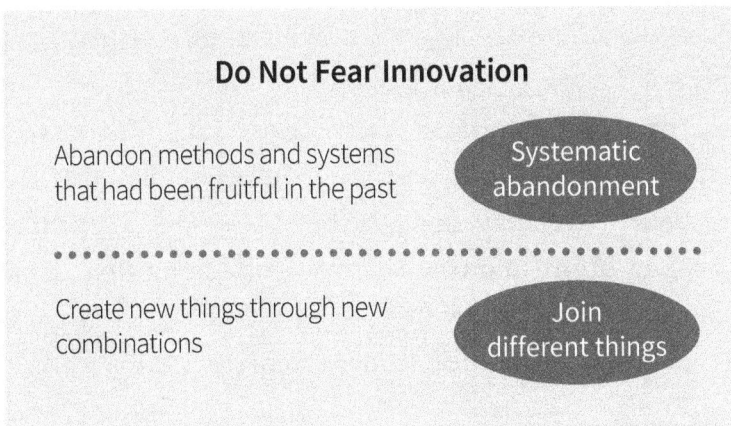

Do Not Fear Innovation

Abandon methods and systems that had been fruitful in the past — Systematic abandonment

Create new things through new combinations — Join different things

is also the process of systematic abandonment, where you abandon methods or systems that no longer produce results.

Government offices require innovation, too

The systems and methods of Japanese government offices have recently been brought into question. The time has come to systematically do away with various ministries and agencies of the central government. It's not a case of tinkering, correcting or adjusting parts of it; we need to thoroughly abandon or scrap entire systems. It is necessary to look at things from the perspective of whether something is really needed, or whether it would be preferable to eliminate it all together.

Most likely, there are a tremendous number of things which can be done away with, which for the most part now only stand in the way of private-sector companies. Previously, government-led efforts to revive Japan from the ashes of defeat in World War II were highly effective. But after the private sector regained strength, this evolved into a system of having to obtain approval for every little thing from some ministry or other. The system, to a large extent, has become one in which various regulations interfere with the work of the private sector.

For that reason, innovation is sorely needed now. Since the citizens feel this acutely in many places, they have strong dissatisfaction with government agencies. Isn't it odd that even as they interfere with the work of the private sector and operate with atrocious efficiency, the bureaucrats should be arrogantly claiming that they require more and more taxes?

Raising taxes might be justified if it contributed to social development and better public administration. Nonetheless, as things now stand, when all we are getting is more bloated government offices and snowballing regulations, it just makes it all the more difficult for the private sector to do business.

As far as our group is concerned, when we wanted to put out a new magazine, we had to obtain prior approval from the Patent Agency just to decide on the name of the magazine. When we went to do that, we were astonished by all the regulations that were involved.

First of all, permission will not be granted if a magazine with a similar name already exists. This holds true even if the magazine with the similar name had been published by a company that no longer exists.

Furthermore, I came up with a magazine name which combined *kanji* [Chinese characters], *katakana* [one form of Japanese syllabary] and English, but the Patent Agency refused to approve it. The agency's response was, "We can't permit this because there's never been anything like it before. Names written in kanji should only use kanji. Katakana has to be katakana. And English has to be English."

Government agencies act in all kinds of strange ways such as this, suppressing the private sector. They make it impossible for the private sector companies to operate effectively and thus reduce their work speed. There are all kinds of government jobs that do just that.

Amidst these conditions, government offices continue their refrain of "We have to raise taxes." This naturally results in a resistance from the private sector. When viewed from the perspective of work theory, this is a natural outcome.

With innovation comes pain

Happy Science is very nimble as far as innovation is concerned, but it is true that innovation entails some very difficult aspects. Since we are discarding what has been very important for us, a factor behind our success or a reason for our good progress, we have internal conflicts between two sides.

In the case of Happy Science, we concentrated on publishing collections of spiritual messages at the start of our activities. But as time went by, we abandoned such methods without any regrets and shifted instead to focus more on my fundamental books*.

In addition, our headquarters, branch offices and so on were all located within rented buildings when we just started. But since we developed so fast, after a while, we switched to a policy of constructing our own buildings and keeping the money in house—this is because a lot of our funds were going to pay rent. This is one form of innovation.

Moreover, the associated costs of public seminars become extremely high once they grow to a certain size. The venue costs can soar if you rent many large ones. Furthermore, since large-scale lecture events and so on are generally held on weekends and holidays, the branch offices become empty because all the members gather at the big event. As a result, everyone ends up gathering at these large venues we had to pay large rental fees for. Therefore, not only do the branches have to pay rent for their own facilities, we also have to pay separate expenses to rent large venues or for satellite broadcast.

In this fashion, an organization experiences heavier uneconomic aspects once it grows beyond a certain size. For that reason, we decided to abandon that approach and switch

---

* The author began recording spiritual messages again since 2010, now totaling over 600 sessions. Many of these have been published as "Spiritual Messages Open Session" series and they amount to over 350 books.

to recording my lectures on videos [DVDs] and showing them at the local branches. So, right now, we have in place a hands-on approach where I give lectures at local branches and satellite broadcasts to reach our overseas followers for major events.

Our organization makes innovations to match our scale at that particular point in time while taking into account various factors and economic effects. This is why, when viewed from someone outside the organization, there are probably some aspects that are difficult to understand.

If you feel that you have reached a limit, you always need to be thinking about how to achieve a breakthrough and make further progress. Nevertheless, you must not forget that with innovation comes pain. Since one aspect of innovation is that you have to abandon what has been effective in the past, pain will inevitably ensue. However, if you want to continue making progress, you have to be ready to accept the fact that such "surgery" may be required at some point.

4

Art of War for the Weak, Art of War for the Strong

Strategies and tactics that are appropriate to The strengths and weaknesses of your organization

Fourth, there are the art of war for the weak and the art of war for the strong. These are important, too. No matter what the organization, if you analyze its characteristics, you will find very few instances in which it will be number one in all aspects. Regardless of the organization or company, you will find certain degrees of strengths and weaknesses.

Consequently, if you consider the strengths of your organization, you will be able to see how you can win with your strengths and how you can cover for your weaknesses, so that they do not cause damage. You must know that all organizations have both strengths and weaknesses.

In addition, by figuring out where your organization or company stands within a certain industry, you can change your tactics. Those organizations where the scale and power are comparatively small in an industry can be considered the "weak," while those where the scale and power are comparatively large are the "strong." So, naturally, how you compete against other organizations will depend on your organization's relative scale and strength.

This aspect of management is extremely delicate and difficult to get a handle on. Managers need to first consider the scale of their organization and establish their strategy based on whether they are a strong party or a weak party. And even after you decide that you are one or the other, you must always remember that your organization has both strong and weak points.

For example, a party may have a lot of capital and may be very strong in terms of accumulated funds, but weak in terms of technology. Conversely, a party may be strong technologically. Or maybe a party is weak in terms of technology and finance, but is very good at promoting its products.

Each organization has its characters and its own strengths and weaknesses. Strategies and tactics need to be devised accordingly.

The Art of War for the weak—
Use your strengths in battle

As a general rule, a weaker party cannot defeat a stronger party in an all-out battle. That is a general principle. There is almost no chance of prevailing if the smaller contends with the larger in an all-out battle.

Consequently, if you conclude that you are the weaker party, then you need to triumph by relying on your strengths. For example, take a small company that is strong only in terms of having superior technology. Perhaps the company has superior technology in a very specific area that a major corporation simply cannot compete in and is therefore outstanding in this very limited area of technology. This kind of company should confine its battle to this area and concentrate its limited resources there.

This is the so-called 'niche industry.' Little crevices in the market that large companies cannot reach are referred to as niches. If you make a thorough attack in such a niche portion, you can enlarge this hole and create a path for growth.

However, if this niche portion grows beyond a certain size, big corporations with a lot of capital will surely get involved and take this market. At that time, the niche company will have to think of the next move: continue to develop in the same area or look for another niche in the market. Those are the approaches available.

The Art of War for a weaker party, basically, is a niche-type strategy that aims for gaps. It is to bore into a niche in the market where stronger parties cannot compete. In other words, it is to launch an unexpected attack.

For instance, the famous warlord Nobunaga Oda used this very strategy during the Battle of Okehazama[*]. His rival Yoshimoto Imagawa had a huge army of 30,000 or 50,000 according to some records, while Nobunaga had merely 2,000 or 3,000 men on his side. In any event, it appears that the odds were at least ten-to-one. Oda's forces would not stand a chance if they fought on flat ground. That was a given. The usual case is, there is absolutely no chance of winning against enemy forces 10 times larger than your own.

Oda's senior retainers declared that they would not stand a chance if they fought head-on and that it would be better to hole up in his castle. Of course, there is no doubt that this strategy, too, would lead to certain defeat.

Under such circumstances, only one strategy offered a chance for victory. In any battle, a large army will have a weak spot—that is where the weaker opponent needs to attack. A

---

[*] A battle fought in Japan in 1560. The lesser army led by Nobunaga Oda defeated the greater army led by Yoshimoto Imagawa. The victory gave Nobunaga a boost; the battle itself was a crucial turning point of the Sengoku [Warring States] period.

large army on the march moves at a slow pace. Furthermore, its line of soldiers extends, meaning that the line becomes thin and stretched out.

The same was true in the period in ancient China described in *The Record of Three Kingdoms*. If a small army fights against a force of a million men in one place, it cannot possibly win. But when an army is on the march, strung out for miles and miles, it will become narrow and spread out; it will be extremely easy to attack one section of it. This is what happened to Liu Bei when he led a large army to avenge the death of his sworn brother-in-arms Guan Yu. He let his line of soldiers get strung out and therefore its center became under attack. Liu Bei was defeated by the forces of the kingdom of Wu.

That was also the strategy adopted by Nobunaga Oda during his miraculous victory at Okehazama. The Imagawa army numbered in the tens of thousands, but it came in a long, narrow formation because it marched along the main highway. The leader of this large army, Yoshimoto Imagawa, was roughly in the middle of the formation, enjoying his lunch exactly at the time of Nobunaga's attack. In addition, it appears to have been raining as his men were taking a break. Since there was only a small group of bodyguards protecting their commander, an attack there, at that moment, ensured victory for Oda.

This was a victorious battle in terms of combat theory, too. Usually, it's very unlikely to win against an enemy force that is 10 times greater than your own. But the number of enemy troops at the point of attack was rather a small force, so a sneak attack on Imagawa's headquarters resulted in victory.

Of course, combat intelligence comes before the actual attack. Since Oda received the news that Imagawa was resting at a certain spot, Oda ordered an attack on that very spot, which amounted to an ambush. He provided the highest military honors to the person who brought him that information. Consequently, even if an opponent has a huge force, concentrating your forces to attack an enemy's weak point can bring you victory.

This principle applies exactly in the same way at the management level. You cannot win against major businesses in an all-out battle. However, such businesses will certainly have their own weak spots. Your company probably has some kind of strengths. If you compete using your strong points, you might win.

Another method for winning is to check where the opponent has spread out thin and attack the chinks in his armor.

That is the Art of War for the weaker party. This, indeed, is how the weak should do battle. If a weaker party fights using its weak points, naturally, it will lose even if it goes for the niche. So, it is important that a weaker party fight with its strongest assets. That is the way to go about things.

The Art of War for the strong—
Encircle with large numbers

On the contrary, the Art of War for the strong involves a strategy in which if the opponent is smaller, you encircle him with a larger force.

Hideyoshi Toyotomi[*] was especially skilled in this tactic. In particular, he often employed this approach once he had become the most powerful man in Japan. He would carefully analyze the forces on his and his enemy's side. If the enemy had just one soldier more than him, he would avoid battle and seek the path of reconciliation or some other political means. If his army outnumbered his enemy's, he wouldn't hesitate to attack. Usually, he would attack using 10 times the number of enemy soldiers. When he attacked Odawara Castle, for example, he attacked with forces 10 times larger than the enemy. When he did that, the enemy's morale

---

* Hideyoshi Toyotomi [ca, 1537 - 1600]: Military commander during the Sengoku period. Born as a son of a peasant, he gained power, unified Japan and was promoted to Kampaku, the chief advisor to the emperor.

plummeted and was able to win without a serious fight, minimizing damage to his own troops.

If you fight with an enemy who is roughly as strong as your side, the damage is going to be tremendous. For example, in a battle between 10,000 soldiers on one side and 12,000 soldiers on the other side, there are going to be a lot of casualties. However, if it is a case of 10,000 men versus 100,000 men, usually the 10,000 will lose their fighting spirit. Weighing their chances, they see that they will lose in no time and therefore surrender without a fight. This is a set pattern and the Art of War of the strong is based on this.

Lanchester's laws

There were a set of laws called 'Lanchester's laws' used during WWII. These were laws applied to air battles. Japan's Zero fighter planes were very strong and the American fighters could not hope to win against the Zero based on performance. When engaged in dogfights, the Zero was very light and extremely maneuverable, it could whip around very quickly. During the first half of WWII, the American side suffered many losses against the Zeros.

The concept that the U.S. came up with to deal with this situation was this: by outnumbering the Zeros three-to-one, their fighters could emerge victorious. The Americans thought that, no matter how technically superior the Zero fighters may be, if they could put three fighters in the air for every Japanese plane, there was no way they could lose. This is obvious. If they enjoyed a three-to-one advantage, that would be the result.

If the U.S. factories could churn out new fighters to the point where the U.S. airmen could go up into the skies with an advantage of three-to-one, then the Americans could annihilate the enemy while suffering almost no damage themselves. A strong industrial power would make this possible.

Even granted that the Zeros were better planes and their pilots first-rate, if the enemy came attacking from three different directions—say from the front, the rear and above—then it would be a case of the better being bested by the many. Generally, there would be no hope for victory.

Even though Japanese fighter pilots were top-notch with 2,000 or 3,000 hours of flying time, they began to get shot down one after the other by the Americans. As a result, the number of seasoned pilots dwindled to a few; the remaining pilots were novices who could easily be knocked out of the skies.

The cream of Japan's pilots were flying these planes, but they were quickly dying off. The Zeros were superior fighter planes, but their numbers continued to fall. Since Japan's production capabilities were inferior, the number of fighter planes continued to decline and, in the end, Japan was beaten to a pulp.

The bottom line is, industrial power is the major factor, so a prolonged war meant no chance of victory for the side with inferior production capabilities. In this way, the American forces used Lanchester's laws with regard to the war in the skies and attacked the Japanese forces with three times their number.

When the American forces attacked an island held by the Japanese forces, they employed this same approach. On the frontlines, the Japanese forces had a total of 100,000 or 300,000 soldiers, depending on the source, but for whatever reason, they were hung up on protecting all the islands and thus scattered their soldiers, here and there.

If all of these 300,000 soldiers had been concentrated at one place, the Japanese side would have enjoyed numerical superiority when the 30,000-strong landing force of the Americans attacked. But since the Japanese forces were loathing to lose even a single island, it dispersed its strength across many islands.

In order to weaken the Japanese forces that were already scattered on different islands, the American forces first took aim at supply ships in order to cut off Japanese supplies.

Sinking civilian supply ships, not just military transports, is actually against international law. At any rate, the American aim was to first sink the supply ships in order to prevent Japanese forces from getting additional supplies. The U.S. forces knew that if this could be done, the Japanese forces would be isolated on the islands.

Let's say there was an island with 10,000 Japanese defenders. The Americans would bring in about 30,000 Marines, so that the odds were three-to-one. Attacking with a three-to-one advantage over the enemy will allow you to completely annihilate its forces.

For example, assume there were 30,000 Japanese troops stationed on three different islands, 10,000 on each. If each island was attacked by 30,000 U.S. troops, one by one and in turns, all Japanese troops will be annihilated. That is what happened to the Japanese forces.

This is the Art of War as practiced by a strong side. Distinguishing the stronger from the weaker, generally speaking, can be done by looking at which side is big and which side is small on the overall scale. Additionally, whether a side is strong or weak could depend on the front where the competition or fight is taking place. You must keep this in mind.

Break the enemy into parts and attack their weak points
By concentrating your forces

In the event that the enemy forces outnumber your own and are stronger, you must split the enemy into smaller components and concentrate your forces on attacking their weak points. Such a strategy is critical.

That is exactly the approach the Prussian forces took in fighting Napoleon. The French forces were always stronger wherever Napoleon led and could not be defeated, but were weak where he did not lead. The Prussians noticed this. They escaped from battles wherever Napoleon appeared. They

---

Art of War for the Weak

- Fight using your strengths
- Find a niche that the strong are least expecting or that they cannot compete in
- Break the enemy into parts and concentrate your attack on their weak points

Art of War for the Strong

- Encircle with large numbers

---

decided that if the French came to attack them, they would retreat after putting up some resistance.

Based on the conventional battle tactic, any retreat signaled defeat. The enemy would pursue, attack and triumph. So, against Prussian forces that would immediately retreat, Napoleon would always come out the winner. However, the Prussians would then reappear in a different place.

The Prussian forces did not see retreat as a loss. Their philosophy was, "We can't beat Napoleon. So, run away if you see Napoleon. Attack the French where Napoleon is not present." Furthermore, they concluded that the French were weak at spots away from Napoleon and that they should attack and destroy the French there. In that way, they whittled down the enemy's strength. The French were strong wherever Napoleon went, but weak elsewhere. On the other hand, the Prussians were weak wherever Napoleon was, but were stronger wherever he wasn't.

In this way, the Prussian forces adopted this tactic of retreating when Napoleon appeared, but seeking to inflict decisive defeats wherever he was not.

Likewise, in ancient China, when Xiang Yu and Liu Bang were vying for supremacy, one of the latter's generals by the name of Han Xin developed the 'ambushes on ten sides' strategy for whittling away little by little the invincible Xiang Yu and his military force. With this strategy, Liu Bang's followers were able to tire out Xiang Yu's army, isolate them in small numbers and encircle them for the kill. This style of fighting is certainly something we need to be aware of.

5

The Theory of Focusing

Invest your business resources on particular subjects

I would like to raise a fifth point, namely the theory of focusing. This is related to Section 4, "Art of War for the Weak, Art of War for the Strong."

In battle, if your forces are quite strong, you may be in a position to fight at full power, all the time, using the maximum force of all sectors and claim victory. But a company, especially one still in the development stage, usually does not have all things readily available.

A company that starts out small usually lacks human resources. Usually, the company will be limited in terms of human resources and capital. Factories and other buildings will be inadequate. For that reason, sometimes start-ups use garages as their production facilities. Apple Computer started out in a garage, too. It's a good example of what I am talking about.

Since a company is small in scale during its earlier stages, it will be lacking in all kinds of business resources. What a company does have, generally speaking, is an idea or the distinguished leadership of the founder. But in terms of manpower, there is only one or two.

As a company grows bigger, it must begin to amass various kinds of business resources. This is an important strategy.

When a company has limited business resources, it will not be able to use the same strategy adopted by larger companies. It will have to be selective and concentrate its meager personnel, material and capital resources on the most effective thing. If the company does not do that, it will not be able to forge a path forward.

No matter how much money you invest into something, if this "something" does not yield profits, it will only be a waste of money. Major businesses with abundant capital can allocate a certain percentage to research on new projects and allow that department to be in deficit. But in a case where a company only has, say, 10 million yen on hand, it would be all over for the company if it spends the 10 million yen on something, only to fail. So, the company has to invest the 10 million yen in something that will give the best results. Otherwise, the company will not succeed. This is the theory of focusing. If management goes all out instead of narrowing down its focus, it will gain only paltry results for the money that they spend.

The Theory of Focusing

Business resources
(people, materials, money, etc.)

Concentrate on the
most effective option

Option

(A) (B) (C) (D) (E) (F) (G)

Managers must be able to both see
the whole picture and focus on a certain point

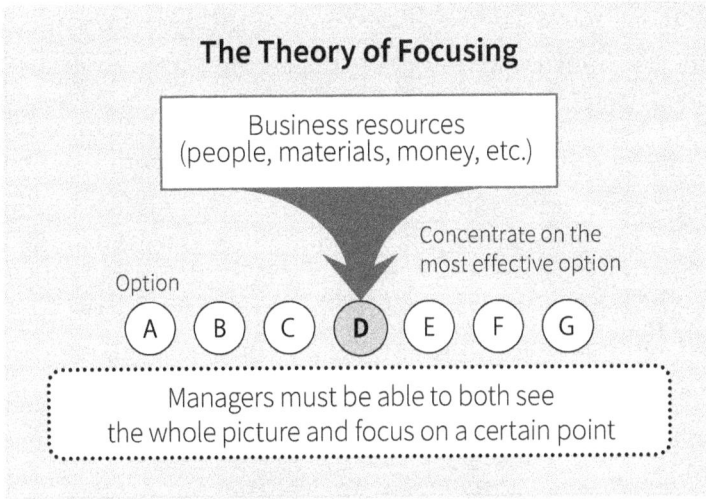

Let me offer some specific examples to explain the situation. For example, the Japanese chain 7-Eleven and many similar convenience stores are in fierce competition with each other. Since the first head of 7-Eleven in Japan was a man of ideas, I understand that in the beginning his intent was to offer around 100 different bento box lunches. His reasoning was that if the store offered many varieties, people in the neighborhood where the stores were located would want to eat one every day. After all, if a consumer ate a different bento every day, then over the course of a year, he would only eat the same bento about three times; the 100 different bentos would surely become a hit.

However, when they put this idea into action, it ended

up in complete failure. If you give a little thought to the matter, I think you can discover the reason for the failure. If a store produces 100 different kinds of bento, customers might well find it fun to try to choose among them, but by making so many varieties available for purchase, the number of each bento sold will be small.

Moreover, making all those different bentos required a lot of work and thus pushed production costs way up. Because the volume of individual ingredients ordered was small, it could not be bought by the bulk. On top of that, in the eyes of a customer, having to choose from among 100 different types could be confusing and bewildering. Those were the defects of the concept.

Then, the company reduced to about 10 of the bestselling types of bento. This improved their revenue tremendously and the bento line was soon in the black. This makes a lot of sense.

For example, if a shop sells a few hundred grilled salmon bentos, it has to buy salmon in bulk. Naturally, the cost price for that particular ingredient will go down. There would be a set procedure to make the bentos. If there are only about 10 different types of bentos to make, then the workers can get very nimble at their tasks, too.

Making 100 different types of bento requires quite a lot of skill. Hiring professionals with the required technical skills is a tremendous undertaking. But if you only need to make items like grilled salmon bentos or grilled meat bentos, then even amateurs will do well enough.

Therefore, by focusing on 10 kinds of bento for sale, the company started gaining profit and succeeded a lot.

In many instances, the founders of companies are full of ideas, so they are the kind of people who come up with one idea after the other. But among those ideas will surely be many which will not turn a profit; rather, such ideas will lead the company into bankrupt due to overwhelming costs.

It is important to come up with new ideas and test them out. Yet, if you conclude that the cost would be too high, you have to focus on something that would likely have the greatest impact.

Narrowing down can apply to exam study

This theory can be applied to other areas as well. Take studying, for example. If you study and study but spread your net too wide, you will end up with scattered knowledge. It will take a very long time for you to be able to raise your real ability.

In Japan, studying for university entrance examinations could be an effort lasting one to three years. Either way, when you think about how much studying you can get done in the time allocated, you will realize that time is limited.

The object of exam study is to achieve the skill level required to pass the exam within a limited amount of time.

I cannot stress enough how important it is to cultivate yourself throughout your life. This is indeed true, however, considering the immediate goal of passing the entrance exam, you have to fulfill the requirements necessary to reach a passing level by, say, the following February or March.

You might do all you can to study subjects that you won't be tested on, but the exam will not measure this kind of academic ability. Consequently, you need to apply the theory of focusing to entrance exams, too.

There are countless educational materials for studying English, but if you wander from book to book, you will not get much result. Even if you have 10 or 20 workbooks, you will only pick at or complete half of each; you will never master them all in only a year.

Of course, you would want to get your hands on as many materials as possible and read them and study them properly. But what you really need to do is to think about which textbook is most appropriate in light of your goal of passing the entrance exam. If you think in terms of the limited period of one year and decide that concentrating on a particular workbook would be your most effective strategy, then you need to focus on that workbook.

If your seniors who have successfully passed or your cram school counselors can point out which educational material is most effective in passing the test, then first devote your entire energy to mastering that material. If you do that, you should be able to reach a passing level without trouble, despite a short period of one year.

On the contrary, if, for example, you want to master the contents of three workbooks, you may not be able to accomplish such a feat. Repetition is critical in building real ability. In order to achieve a certain level, repeat three times, five times or as many times as it takes you. You won't be able to raise your scores if you are always moving on to tackle new questions. Please understand this point well.

Test takers from outside of cities, who do not have ready access to information about the tests, often fail because of this. Students who live in areas where a great deal of information about the exams are exchanged will be in the loop and stand a good chance of passing, while those living in areas where information is scarce are more likely to fail.

Furthermore, students who failed the university entrance exams and are spending time studying until the next exam without attending cram schools, should also know that this is one of the reasons for their failure. As they have all day to study, they think that they have an unlimited amount of time and purchase various kinds of educational materials and reference books and overly widen their area of study. As a result, even a further year of such study proves to be insufficient and they gain little, only to end up failing the exams again.

However, at cram schools, the study materials used in instruction are surprisingly thin. That is because cram schools realize that the test takers do not have the time to devour loads of educational materials and have to focus. Therefore, if they can really ingest the content of these thin study materials, the students would gain a sense of achievement. And through constant repetition, they would memorize the contents well.

In a similar fashion, it is essential to focus on the important parts if the main aim is to get results in a short time. This is what you must do.

Two perspectives necessary of managers

Although this method is not directly related to whether people will enjoy final victory in their life, this method will undoubtedly prove helpful in clearing the bars at various turning points in life. When deadlines are involved, focusing becomes essential.

On the other hand, when it comes to things that do not involve deadlines, I believe you need to give your best in a variety of fields.

In management, we have the final settlement or closing of the books. Managers are always concerned with how they can stay out of the red during a given business term. They know, for example, that if a bill for payment is not honored, they may be in deep trouble for the business year. When faced with such a situation, they concentrate and do everything possible to avoid such an unfavorable outcome.

However, when judged from a long-term perspective, they must think about the long-term development and prosperity of the firm. Therefore, they must be interested in and conduct research concerning a wide range of areas.

In this fashion, it is necessary to view things both from a long-term, broad perspective as well as in a short-term, focused perspective. One must be like a hawk that can view from a distance while, at the same time, be able to concentrate all his energy on pursuing a prey after spotting it. One must be able to look at things from both perspectives.

Managers, in particular, must have a wide-angled perspective and a microscopic perspective, so that they can view carefully and analyze a point from both an expanded perspective and in detail. They will fare poorly if they don't have both of these faculties. Having only one perspective will not suffice.

Technically-oriented individuals can easily focus on a certain point, but in many cases they won't be able to see the whole picture. Conversely, some people can grasp the overall situation but are incapable of focusing on a single point. If you are like a commentator who has rough knowledge about many topics, but does not understand how to concentrate on investing capital, you may make a fine commentator but a lousy manager.

This, too, can be considered an Art of War. If you were to think of your life in definite periods rather than in abstract terms of some decades, then you will need to apply the law of concentration to your affairs.

6

The Theory of Attacking in Waves

Jumping from the crest of one wave to the next

The sixth point I want to address is the theory of attacking in waves. What flourishes must decline after reaching its peak. In Buddhism, this is referred to as the impermanence of all things. It holds true no matter what you are talking about, whether it be physical exercise, study, the arts or physical strength; once a peak has been reached, decline follows as surely as night follows the day.

Applying this principle to business, we see that selling a certain product when its sales are on the upswing will produce a lot of profit and will make the company grow. However, that product will inevitably reach its peak in sales.

Since it is a fixed law that things will inevitably reach their peak, you should know of this law beforehand. Whether the peak comes one year later, three years later or five years later, depends on the type of product, but there will surely come a peak. Consequently, you must be able to estimate when it will come.

The Theory of Attacking in Waves

Sales

Things will inevitably reach their peak

Product A   Product B   Product C   Product D

Time

Predict the wave cycle and
prepare the next wave beforehand

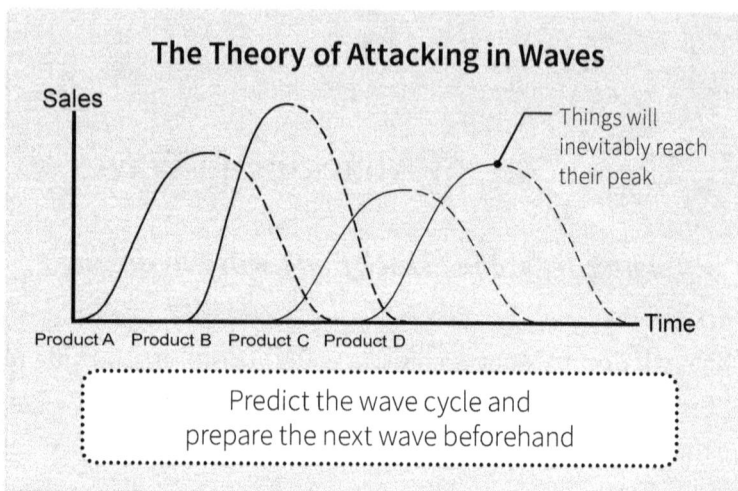

A peak, if we describe it in terms of a diagram, is like the crest of a wave. A peak will surely come and the decline will commence after that.

Even if a new product is put on sale and sells well, other products will appear that cut into sales and the product will disappear. This is only natural. You could come up with a new product and it could become a hit, but if a lot of similar products flood the market and the competition gets fierce, the product may whittle away. These things surely occur.

If your company only has one product, then there will only be one peak. Relying on a single peak is a very risky thing to do in terms of company operations—if you have to support a large number of staff over the long term of several decades. Therefore, you have to create the next wave before you reach the crest of the current product. The crest of the next wave must come a while after the crest of the first wave. Make sure that the crest of that next wave will come in a few years' time. When that happens, you will always end up jumping from one wave crest to the next. We can call this the theory of attacking in waves.

Since everything will reach its peak, you should predict the wave cycle and prepare the next wave as much as you can.

Making huge waves

Please keep this in mind: if a wave cycle is too short, the profit or outcome of that wave will diminish, so you have to be careful in this regard.

For instance, our organization had the goal of proving the authenticity of spiritual messages in our early days, so we published spiritual messages at a rapid pace of one book every two weeks.

We produced them at such a fast clip that, while the books would be on the bestseller list, when the next book came out, it would bump the previous one from the bestseller list. In our early days, every time we published a new book, it would sell about 15,000 copies within two weeks. But as we pressed on and immediately put out the next book, the preceding publication would drop in sales while the new one would sell well.

In this case, the waves were a bit too small and too close to each other. We were too eager to get the next book out. When we decided to issue new books at a pace of every two or three months to create larger waves, each would sell 50,000, 100,000 or even 200,000 copies whereas one book previously sold around 15,000 copies.

If there is a product that you believe will be a hit-item, you need to think in terms of big waves. If you intend to go big once or twice a year, you have to work to make each wave last for a long time.

For example, if a book is skillfully sold for a year and becomes a good seller, usually that means sales of 200,000 or 300,000 copies. In comparison, if you only have a month to sell the book, the number of sales will not be so high.

Thus, in order to have a long-term, large wave, you have to bear in mind its connection to other books you intend to publish. It's not about getting out there as many titles as possible. In the event that you are offering a book that should sell several hundred thousand copies, it's OK to also publish other books that you figure would sell 30,000 to 50,000 copies. But if you put out bestseller contenders in quick succession, you may actually see the market shrinking.

Making long-selling products

The lifespan of books are as I have described just now. In the case of other items, sometimes they have a longer lifespan. Some products will sell well for three years. Some, like Datsun motor* vehicles in the old days, would continue to sell well for an extended period. Or take the extreme case of the *Oronamin C* health drink that first appeared at the time of the 1964 Tokyo Olympics and still continues to sell well.

If you can come up with such a long-selling product, your earnings are certain to be very good. If you can just offer one long-selling product or a long hit, your business will be extremely stable, but such a product rarely comes by. If you can offer something like that, a single hit can create a large company.

What's scary is that a company whose products proved big can bring demise to its own hit by putting out similar products.

This is how the theory of attacking in waves works. Since all things have their own peak, you must think about when the peak is likely to arrive and prepare the next wave. You have to think about the second wave and the third wave.

If you look at the history of Happy Science, you can see that we have used this tactic to a considerable extent. We are always thinking about what to do next and what to do after the next as we launch our wave attacks.

---

* A famous Japanese automobile brand that produced cars to the public mainly from 1930s to 1970s.

7

The Theory of Promotion

The seventh topic is the theory of promotion. The term *promotion* sounds as though it has to do with businesses, but in reality, promotion is a concept that originated in religion. Religion is the true source of promotion.

In a sense, religion is all about promotion. Since the whole purpose of an organized religion is to figure out how to spread teachings and doctrines through promotional activities, promotion is the very mission of religion. Although you might think of promotion as a business-related thing, it definitely has a religious side to it, too.

If we look back at religions in the past, we can easily understand that the theory of promotion was expressed within them. Since in ancient times there were no newspaper ads or TV commercials, unlike today, promotion was a very thorny issue.

For example, the Passion of Jesus Christ was definitely a case of promotion. Although human beings do not react strongly to favorable news, they show excessive response to unfavorable news, tragedies or scandals. When we hear bad news, such as someone having died, the reaction is 10 times as intense as when we hear good news.

Human beings are destined to die; someone dies somewhere, every single day. Although human death is nothing out of the ordinary, human beings are hardwired to have excessive reactions to bad news.

The fact that Jesus was crucified on the cross was truly something earth-shattering. However, in terms of the theory of promotion, we can see that this was a way of doing promotion given that there were no funds.

'Dying by crucifixion' was a great scandal at the time, so it received a lot of attention. Average people, by their very nature, cannot tell good from bad, so they will think,

Examples of Promotion in Religion

Buddhism
(Shakyamuni
Buddha's Order)

- Over 1,000 renunciant disciples
- A shaved head and a saffron robe
- Kings and others of high status as followers

Christianity

- The Passion of Christ
- The sign of the cross
- Ninety-Five Theses by Martin Luther

"Everyone's talking about it, so although I don't understand it, it must be something amazing." Thus the cross became a kind of promotion.

After that, people such as St. Paul emerged as a Christian theorist. He developed theories to give meaning to the death of Jesus. Saint Paul stated that Jesus was crucified to atone for the sins of human beings. He came up with the concept of atonement and established the theoretical basis for explaining the event.

Thus, Christians adopted the sign of the cross as their own and spread their faith throughout the entire world. This, too, can be considered as a method of promotion.

Furthermore, contemporary analysis reveals that Buddha's Sangha, too, did quite a lot of promotional work. Buddha's Sangha had a tremendous number of renunciant disciples, so running the order must have been very difficult. At times, an entire religious group was converted to Buddha's order, leading to as many as 1,000 new people joining Buddha's Sangha as renunciant disciples and subsisting on alms. Understandably, receiving alms must have been tough.

When dozens or hundreds of renunciant disciples with their shaved heads and saffron colored robes came down together from Vulture Mountain with their alms bowls, they must have looked like an army. They probably made the impression that Buddha's Sangha was a very large organization or order. Consequently, having many disciples also played a large role in promotion, as it showed that the Sangha was a very large one.

Furthermore, Buddha's followers also included kings and other converts of high status. That, too, served as a form of promotion for the group. I believe such methods are used by contemporary religions as well.

Returning to Christianity, there is the case of Martin Luther, who used the sensational method of promotion of posting his Ninety-Five Theses onto the front door of the castle church at Wittenberg.

So, in this fashion, promotion is employed in various ways in the field of religion. The methods employed have greatly affected how much a religion has spread. Therefore, we cannot necessarily say that promotion is a theory that is only applicable to businesses.

8

Marketing Theory—
Become Customer-Oriented

Marketing methods as evident
In Kamakura Buddhism

The eighth point is marketing theory. Looking at the field of religion through the lens of management analysis, we can say that religions have engaged quite extensively in marketing, even in the past.

That is especially true if we look at the methods used to spread Kamakura Buddhism*. In the case of Kamakura Buddhism, the emphasis shifted from the religious style to seek individual enlightenment to mass spreading of the faith among the common people. So, in contemporary terms, we get the distinct impression that marketing-style methods were utilized.

---

* A reformation movement in Japanese Buddhism during the Kamakura period [end of 12th century - early 14th century]. Until then, Buddhism had an academic and noble taste to it, however, new sects of Buddhism became more popular among samurais and farmers.

For example, Shinran[*] ignored difficult Buddhist theory and claimed that all that was required for salvation was to chant *Namu Amida Butsu*[†]. This is an extremely simplified method of spreading faith.

Not only that, but he also put forward the doctrine that bad people, in particular, can be saved. The usual case would be to say that good people can be saved while bad people cannot be saved, as according to the law of cause and effect. Shinran took the following position: "No, saying only good people can be saved is equivalent to saying that Buddha has little mercy. The fact that bad people, in particular, will be saved is proof of Buddha's great compassion." Shinran preached that one could be saved by chanting Namu Amida Butsu, no matter how bad a person he may be.

Moreover, he added that it was not necessary to recite Namu Amida Butsu tens of thousands or millions of times. He said that merely wanting to recite is enough for you to be saved. In this way, he made it easier and easier.

Here, we can see that Shinran made good use of a method to expand his marketing target. One of the bottlenecks to the propagation of Buddhism undoubtedly had been

---

[*] Shinran [1173 - 1262]: A Buddhist monk who lived in the early Kamakura period and founded *Jodo Shinshu* [True Pure Land Buddhism].

[†] It means, "I put my faith in Amitabha Buddha [the Buddha of Infinite Light]."

the impression that the sutras were difficult. The Chinese language in which they were written were certainly difficult to fathom for the average person. Moreover, Buddhist monks read them in a special way of reading that the average person knew nothing about. It was not the usual way of reading; it was a difficult way of pronunciation known as *go-on*, that is to say, Sinicized readings with the style of pronunciation common in Southern China at that time.

As such, the difficulty of the sutras allowed Buddhist monks to make a living off explaining the sutras. However, as far as the spreading of Buddhism was concerned, this situation represented a distinct bottleneck. For that reason, Shinran decided to skip what mattered more: the content of the sutras.

In addition, although Buddhism had taught that bad people could not be saved, Shinran's contention that even bad people could be saved was an attempt to gain even more converts.

Nowadays, believers in the Jodo Shinshu sect established by Shinran are officially said to number more than 10 million. But seeing how little it takes to be considered a member, it is impossible to get an accurate account of the number of believers. If that manner of counting is to be accepted, it would be very difficult to say how many believers our own group has. Anyway, I believe there are at least tens of millions of them.

Shinran simplified the teachings to such an extent and developed his theory as a way to create a bigger market for the teachings.

The propagation method developed by Nichiren[*] was quite similar. Nichiren concluded that because of the large number of sutras existing, everyone could not learn them all. He therefore preached the superiority of the Lotus Sutra that had been popularized by the Chinese monk, T'ien-t'ai Chih-i[†]. Nichiren claimed that the Lotus Sutra alone was sufficient and that he could not be mistaken since that is what Chih-i said. However, since the content of the Lotus Sutra was complicated and difficult to comprehend, he said that simply repeating the line, *Namu Myoho Renge Kyo*[‡] would be sufficient.

In comparing Namu Amida Butsu with Namu Myoho Renge Kyo, we can see that the lengths of the two phrases are about the same. They were a fair match in the rivalry between the two groups during that period.

I would also point out that Nichiren was intolerant of other Buddhist sects, declaring among other things that Zen was the work of a devil, Shingon would destroy the nation

---

[*] Nichiren [1222 – 1282]: A Buddhist monk who lived in the early Kamakura period and founded *Nichirenshu* [Nichiren Buddhism].

[†] T'ien-t'ai Chih-i [538 – 597]: A Chinese Buddhist monk who systemized the teachings of Tiantai Buddhism. He categorized and analyzed the vast teachings of Shakyamuni Buddha and saw the Lotus Sutra as the highest teaching of Buddhism.

[‡] It means, "I put my faith in the Lotus Sutra."

and believers in other sects would be flung into Hell, all since the Lotus Sutra was the sole road to salvation.

From a contemporary perspective, we can say that Nichiren had adopted a strategy of differentiation, declaring that his way was the only glorious way and that it was totally different from all other ways. He told those segments of the population that held different beliefs, "If you persist in believing as you do, you are destined for Hell." You can probably feel how he was calling out to attract "customers" by warning them to abandon their existing beliefs and saying that his message alone promised salvation.

In contemporary terms, we can say that this resembled a sales war among different companies. For example, Panasonic and Hitachi make the same kinds of home appliances. It would be like a Panasonic salesperson declaring, "If you use Hitachi products, you are headed straight for Hell. But if you use Panasonic products, you will go to Heaven." This is extreme.

Back then, Japan's total population probably numbered in the tens of millions. Even so, recognizing that the number of potential customers was limited, the leaders of various sects were battling to see how they could gain adherents for their own.

Compared to this easy path of sects emphasizing faith, the Zen sect preached a more difficult path.

Dogen*, the founder of the Soto sect of Zen, wrote many long books. What exactly do you get if you boil down Dogen's Zen to its essence? I get the distinct feeling that he never reached enlightenment. In the end, he simply came to the conclusion that Zen is to sit in meditation [*zazen*].

Zen is said to be a difficult path. Even so, Dogen's method was to create a style of zazen meditation and invite people to participate in it. That was his attempt to spread the faith to the masses.

Furthermore, in the past, Buddhism had taught that it was more difficult for a woman, than a man, to be saved. It was told that women had many impediments to enlightenment and thus difficult for a woman to return straight to Heaven. That was because a woman had many impediments in the form of family and children; when she married into another family, she had to deal with her mother-in-law and father-in-law, which also created impediments. In addition, there were other impediments related to a woman's physiology. All of which made it difficult for women to be saved.

Looking at the Lotus Sutra, we can see it speaking of women returning to Heaven only after becoming men. This is the concept of "masculinized women."

---

* Dogen [1200 - 1253]: A Zen Buddhist monk who lived in the early Kamakura period and founded *Sotoshu* [Soto school of Zen Buddhism].

This kind of thinking did exist, but Dogen declared as he spread the zazen style, "Women and men are the same if they perform zazen. What impediments can there be for women?" and got rid of that part of the teachings. If you allow women into a market previously restricted to men only, you will double the market size.

Therefore, if we look back at these styles of missionary work during the Kamakura period, we get the distinct impression that all the various sects were vying with each other in terms of how to employ marketing techniques. I believe marketing techniques are nothing new to our age; they have been around for ages.

Discovering demand and creating demand

Let's apply this method to contemporary business theory. We would get the idea, "how to discover and expand segments of the population who will purchase our products."

This is a consumer-oriented way of thinking. You have to spot consumer needs. Not only do you need to discover them, next you need to create needs. You want customers to think to themselves, "I never realized up until now that such a wonderful product existed." Here, you are creating new needs.

What happened back in the Kamakura period was that Buddhist disciples went out to teach the grace of Namu Myoho Rengekyo or Namu Amida Butsu to people who, up until then, had little idea of its grace.

If we analyze Buddhism of the Kamakura era from the standpoint of capturing new customers, we can see that this was a case of not just discovering demand but creating demand, too. These spiritual leaders were clearly engaged in a process of creating demand.

However, what is different from today is that, at the time, roughly 99 percent of the Japanese people believed in the other world and that they would be sent to Hell if they committed evil deeds. Of course, the spiritual leaders went about their work under such premises. This makes it a little different from the situation we have today.

In this fashion, the theory of how to attract the most customers has permeated religion, too. Although there may be some slight conceptual differences, the ways of going about this task are pretty much the same. Various religious groups are engaged in competition to secure believers, even today.

There are various indices used within businesses, for example, turnover, earnings power, number of employees, number of factories and so on. Moreover, there are various indices specific to each industry.

For religions, the most important index is the number of members. A religious group with a large number of believers would be comparable to a major business. Each religion or sect is involved in the same quest to increase its fellowship.

The end result is that in order to increase the number of believers, religions tend to increasingly simplify their doctrines and simplify their methodology for spiritual training. In this way, without even being aware of it, religions have been undertaking promotional campaigns to spread their teachings for a very long time.

In the case of Happy Science, seeing from the perspective of contemporary theory, one of our challenges is to discover demand.

In the past, people generally believed in spirits and the other world and feared falling to Hell, but nowadays, we have

Marketing Theory

Discovering demand	Creating demand
Research customer needs	Tell customers why they need your product
If a market already exists	If a market does not exist

quite a lot of people who are atheists. So, the issue becomes how to discover demand among this class of people.

What's more, another aspect we have to consider is the creation of demand. As far as religious groups are concerned, they, of course, have to establish as an indicator how they can create new demand in such people.

This is a general theory also applicable to businesses. When a company wants to introduce a new product, it is extremely important that the company first discover whether or not there will be demand for that product. Next, it is important to decide whether it can create new demand.

At the moment, the mainstream of Western marketing theory thinks in the following way: consumers are very smart, so if you put out a product that consumers want, it will sell. In terms of political theory, this clearly resembles democratic thinking. The thinking that voters are smart and will make smart choices is reflected in the similar thinking that consumers are smart, will make smart choices and buy good products.

However, one has to have certain doubts as to whether such conclusions are really correct or not. For instance, there was no demand for the electric light bulb before Thomas Edison invented it. It was precisely because he made that discovery that the demand was first created. It was something that had not previously existed, but came into being at a certain point in time. If you had asked someone if he wanted electric light bulbs prior to Edison's invention, you would not find anyone who would say that he did.

In this way, a new product will become a necessity and be popularized because manufacturers conclude as such. There are many cases like this.

The same holds true for railways. Only the rather outstanding individuals realized why there was a need for railways before they were invented. At first, most people do not have the slightest idea. In the past, people looked at their horses, thought about how they could ride them anywhere as long as they were fed and concluded that horses were more convenient than trains. When you had fine horses readily available, where on earth was the need to go out of your way to introduce steam-breathing monsters or heavy hunks of iron to run through the countryside?

Moreover, in order to create a railway, you have to lay hundreds of kilometers of track because the trains can only run on the track. No wonder people initially found railways to be very inconvenient.

For that reason, all kinds of debate took place before the train tracks were laid. Opposing groups offered arguments such as, "If you have a horse, you have the freedom to take any highway or byway" or "If a railway was laid, it would destroy the livelihoods of people who earn their living through horse-related jobs."

They castigated the railways as inconvenient and bizarre and said all kinds of disparaging things. They could not imagine, in any way, that the railways would cause such tremendous revolutions in transportation.

It was the same story with the airplane. No one could believe that such a vehicle could actually fly in the sky. For people living in the 19th century, the idea that a metal mode of conveyance could soar through the heavens was inconceivable. If someone had carried out a market survey at that time, asking if the public wanted to fly in a metal carriage up in the sky, no one would have said yes. The very thought of flying about in the sky was scary; they did not want to die. They would surely have thought they were being deceived.

Market-oriented thinking is important, but in the case of something completely new, there will often be no preexisting market. There are times when genius inventors and entrepreneurs create their own markets—in such times, they cannot depend solely on going around and talking to consumers to discover demand.

However, at the stage where a certain level of needs have appeared, you have to go about creating new products while keeping a close eye on consumer trends.

In economics there is something known as Say's Law, named after the French economist Jean-Baptiste Say [1767-1832]. Say's Law is a very primitive principle that says supply can create its own demand; in other words, "If you supply something, it will sell." I believe modern history can be seen as evidence of this principle in action.

Let's say somebody comes up with something that had not existed up until that point and begins to sell it. Take the radio, for example. At first, consumers wondered what this apparatus could possibly do. But once they knew how to use the radio, everybody went out to purchase one. The same thing happened with cars and television.

Accordingly, at the time of a new invention, it is probably true that if you make something, it will sell. However, in the case of television, once numerous models had appeared and various companies had started to enter the marketplace, the "make it and it will sell" maxim no longer held true. In that case, you would be bested if you didn't offer TV models that appealed to more customers.

This is why manufacturers now have to conduct surveys to determine consumer preferences regarding size, price, color, design and various other features. They have to constantly conduct surveys to determine what is in demand as far as TVs are concerned at the moment.

Now, there are wall-mounted TVs. This reflects the concept of TV as an integral part of a room's interior design, a concept that had not existed until now. Previously, the focus had been on the quality of the picture, so TVs tended to be heavy, bulky, black and not very attractive. But now, there is a type to be mounted on a wall.

In a case like this, it is difficult to definitively declare whether it is a case of discovering demand or creating demand.

Oftentimes a market will not exist until a new product is introduced. However, after the item is introduced into the market, you next have to find out the tastes of the consumers or clients and match those preferences in order to supply new products that will receive a good market response. It is critical that you always keep an eye on trends among the users of the product.

9

Emphasizing Product Strength— Don't Skimp on Research and Development

R&D and Marketing are two sides of the same coin

The ninth point I would like to discuss is emphasis on product strength. Regarding this point, as in the last section, it is imperative to always investigate consumer trends. Little wonder there is a business maxim: "Even with the same product, it will sell well if you can enhance marketing power." However, to begin with, a young company will never grow if it lacks product strength. Whether the product suits the era is also a factor.

Take Toyota Motors for instance. Back in the days of Sakichi Toyoda[*], the forerunner company was in the business of manufacturing textile looms. Then in the era of his son, Kiichiro Toyoda, it began to research and build motor vehicles. In this case, they were responding to both making products with product appeal and being in tune with the era.

---

[*] Sakichi Toyoda [1867 – 1930]: A Japanese inventor and entrepreneur, who is the founder of the Toyota Group.

In this way, when a business is newly developing, usually, it first has to identify what its products will be. At the beginning, when it is probably lacking both personnel and capital and has practically nothing at all, it must have a product. When it starts selling is when a company usually gets on a firm footing.

Consequently, it is extremely important to keep working on research and development. When pursuing R&D, you need to do intensive research in order to come up with a totally new product. But at the same time you must never forget the needs of those who will be using the product, as you must do in marketing.

Same thing applies to Happy Science lecturers giving lectures. If lecturers, who are on the supply side, think only of themselves, they will probably think about just speaking in the allotted amount of time since they have been assigned the role. However, if lecturers can stop to consider things from the standpoint of the listeners, they would imagine what kind of topics the audience wants to hear when putting together the content of their lecture. Furthermore, they would want to listen to the impressions of the audience after the lecture, so that they could find out where they need to make improvements. They would ponder how they should improve their lecture for the next time.

R&D and customer-oriented marketing, in a certain sense, are two sides of the same coin. In the beginning, when a new product is being born and during the process when it is being distributed and consumed, it is essential to see whether the product is liked and what the reactions to it are, so that constant improvements can be made. The difficulty is that even if you have a fine product, without a doubt, competitive products will appear.

It is a bit unusual for products like Coca Cola and Pepsi Cola, companies which are quite similar, to coexist. Both of these companies aggressively compete in terms of marketing. For example, they conduct blind taste comparisons, asking participants to choose which drink they think tastes better.

But the first thing is the product. Although in the beginning Coca Cola had a pronounced medicinal taste to

Tips on R&D

☐ Keep in mind the needs of the users who will be using your product

☐ Check customer reactions and make constant improvements

☐ If you are not achieving results equivalent to your development costs, wait for the market to mature and grow before selling your product

it, it sold very well after improvements. Things can develop in that manner. The product in question might be either tangible items or software or intangible concepts. Either way, it is essential to think that coming up with new products is highly valuable.

Microsoft is an example of a company that grew very rapidly. Its computer software products like Windows sold in large quantities because the product had substantial sales power. Bill Gates' idea was to make Microsoft products the industry standard. He stated that no matter how fine the technology was, it could be sold in huge volumes only if it were made the industry standard and made it easy for everyone to use. Computers went from being operated by hitting keys on the keyboard to operating with the use of the mouse. In this way, the emphasis should be to look at things from the standpoint of the customer and make the product easier to use.

Another approach is to wait for the market to mature and grow to a certain size before selling a product, even after doing extensive R&D. Unless a market somewhat matures, you cannot expect to achieve results equivalent to your development costs. For example, here I would note that this is sometimes criticized as a "second-hand sales method" since the method amounts to a strategy of letting other companies do the heavy lifting to develop a market to a certain size before offering a better product or easier-to-use product for sale. Matsushita Electric, before it changed its name to Panasonic, was labeled as a business that indulged in this second-hand sales approach. After all, it is easier to start selling into a market that has already been created by someone else.

You run the risk of failing if you're the first one to try something. But you are less likely to fail if you already know that your product will sell. Furthermore, if you can improve on the idea and make it easier to use so that customers may better love it and make it the standard, you will be able to sell huge quantities of it.

If you can "dock" the R&D elements and marketing elements, you will be able to sell on a grand scale and in large volume. Do that and your profits should swell. This is the kind of thinking that you need to have. Selling only small amounts of your product will not expand sales nor will it make a profit.

Profits can speed up progress

Making a profit can increase the speed of your progress. For example, religions are public organizations and not profit-oriented so, as a matter of course, it does not operate according to the concept of profit. However, they do have to have items equivalent to profit in their accounts. These are costs incurred for the sake of developing and continuing their operations.

If the level of profits become large, say to the level where a religious organization can build its own buildings, and if that profit continues to get larger, then the religion may, for example, be able to make its own movies. This will not be possible if the level of profits is low.

Public organizations and other non-profit organizations do not operate based on the concept of profits, but they still need capital to develop or to cover their costs. The better foundation they have, the faster their pace of progress. So, even non-profit organizations need to have this kind of thinking. And the method they use to achieve that goal is to put out "software" to attract as many people as possible. They have to keep in mind that their "product" will make a lot of people happy. Thus, it is vital to combine R&D and marketing.

10

The Logic of "Shallow, Wide and Long"

Digging too deep can stifle development

The tenth point I want to raise is the logic of "shallow, wide and long." This is something that we, too, are very careful about in our organization. The mistake, trap or pitfall that nearly all new religions end up in is that they dig too deep.

From the standpoint of management theory, this would be poor product appeal. When you have a good product, it will sell well widely. But if your product is not that good, then you are only going to attract a few customers and will tend to dig too deep, which means that you will try to get all you can out of each customer. This is almost always true of fraudulent businesses selling goods that claim to bring good luck or give supernatural benefits.

This is a matter of management skills, too. When you want to spend a lot of money but have few customers, you inevitably take too much from each one. For example, let's take the case of Religion A*. Let's leave its value as a religion

---

* The author is referring to *Aum Shinrikyo*, a new religious movement founded in Japan in 1987 that was responsible for the 1995 Tokyo subway sarin gas attack.

aside for now and analyze it purely in terms of business administration.

Apparently, at the zenith of its popularity, Religion A had more than 10,000 believers, of whom roughly 1,000 had become renunciant disciples. I understand that this number had grown to 1,700 in their final days. They must have been quite desperate in their last stages.

Having 1,700 renunciant disciples out of 10,000 believers means one renunciant disciple in every six believers. That fact alone is enough to theoretically show that the group would collapse. The livelihoods of such a large number of ordained members could not be sustained by such a small group of lay members. With a normal religion, there might be one priest for every 100 members. This is the general rule. So, if the ratio is one in every six, there's no way the religion can sustain itself. In such a situation, what would happen is that the religion will take extreme measures; lay members would be deprived of their entire property.

From a management viewpoint, this is the height of foolishness. Fraudulent businesses where they sell items that they claim to have spiritual benefit use the same method. Let's take a group, Association T*, for instance. The fact that it doesn't really have a reliable product to begin with is hindering its growth. That group has published hardly any

---

* The author is referring to the Unification Church [*Toitsu Kyokai* in Japanese], a new Christian religious movement that originated in South Korea.

books or other literature and only has one video. Since the association doesn't have any products to promote its message, it had to come up with a great many techniques to deceive people. As a result, believers have been subjected to severe suffering.

The founder wanted to spend big money and invested a tremendous amount of it into businesses in South Korea. However, since the association doesn't have its own products to generate an income from, its adherents peddle seals and vases. So, in that way the association has tried to come up with ways that would generate lots of profits, but it all has a pitiful feel to it. Applying pure management analysis, we can see that Association T is pushing people too far and, as a result, its believers are the ones suffering.

People didn't join that religion to go around selling personal seals or to be told to peddle "Treasure Pagodas." Of course, if there were religious legitimacy in spreading those items, that would be fine. If the association's teachings clearly stated that personal seals are absolutely essential to the attainment of enlightenment or that these special pagodas had great significance, then there would be no problem because it would be logically legitimate. But this is not the case; believers are simply going about trying to raise funds.

In that sense, despite not having a good product, the association unreasonably seeks to collect funds. That is why you get such fraudulent hucksterism, which falsely promises spiritual benefits. In this regard, the religion is digging too deep—it is taking too much of what they shouldn't be taking in the first place.

There was also a religious group that charged millions of yen [tens of thousands of dollars] for attendance at training sessions. This, too, can be considered an example of digging deep for money. The fact that the group had to go such extremes to get money proved that it lacked popularity. Since that religion was not popular, it had to milk the few participants as much as possible.

This is based on the assumption that the participants will not come back, so the objective is to take as much as possible from them the first time around. But the fact that the religion is taking millions of yen from participants has become a problem. The group has drilled a bit too deep. If it had a customer-oriented mentality, it would never do such a thing. But the group insists on a producer-oriented mentality, not one that cares for the customer. If the producer side is preoccupied with only its own interests, then its sense of values will contradict with that of the customers, which easily gives rise to trouble. If groups like this were truly religious organizations, the emphasis would be on retaining believers for a long period of time. They should not be trying to kill the golden goose every time it shows up.

Another example is a religious group with a very low retention rate that takes its members for all they are worth in just two or three months. The members are then left to decide whether they want to stay or leave. The groups that have been causing trouble usually have such kind of thinking. Since they are only interested in spending the money, they must think of their believers as nothing more than useful tools. This, I believe, is a stance that eventually precludes any chances for their development.

Good merchandise that Many people can use for a long time

The principle of "shallow, wide and long" can also be applied to taxes. If taxes are too high, the citizens will stop working. If taxes become exorbitant, say, "50 percent for the government, 50 percent for the people" or "60 percent for the government, 40 percent for the people," the people will lose their motivation and stop working. So, it won't do to make taxes too high.

On the other hand, if the tax rates are too low, tax revenue will decline. Then, if you set the tax rates at around 10 percent or 20 percent and encourage the citizens to work throughout their life, the nation will become stable and will develop. If you collect a lot of taxes each year, the citizens will become exhausted and the nation will decline.

In addition, it is necessary to spread a wide net in collecting taxes. However, under the current tax system of Japan, a lot of taxes come from where it is easy to get the money, while nothing is collected from other areas. In order to correct this situation, the government is considering to increase the consumption tax, but the right way to go about collecting taxes is to collect a small amount of taxes from many different areas, which is in line with the "shallow and wide" philosophy.

Furthermore, taxes must be collected over a long period of time. For example, if the government one year decided to squeeze the last penny out of the citizens and killed them by starvation, the government will be unable to collect taxes next year. In other words, the tax load has to be spread over a long period of time.

That is the situation at the national level. The same thing holds true for companies. Companies have to cultivate steady customers who will become repeat purchasers of your products. For example, some companies might be tempted to sell one light bulb for hundreds of thousands of yen, but this method is similar to that of shady religious groups. If a religious group taught, "Buy one of these light bulbs. Once in a lifetime opportunity. You will enjoy happiness until the

The Principle to Make Your Business Grow

Shallow ··· Offer good things at affordable prices

Wide ··· To as many people as possible

Long ··· Have people use those things for a long time

light bulb gives out," it would surely become a fraudulent business.

Nevertheless, a light bulb is sure to give out after a few hundred hours. Therefore, if you can get customers to come back after the light bulb gives out and have them buy their next light bulb from you, they would be your repeating customers. This would be better. And if you offer them good products, they will recommend your company to other people. That is the key to spreading your sales net.

Some people aim to make killer profits by offering something unusual, but the outcome is usually unsuccessful. In the end, the principle for making your business grow is to offer good products, so that many people will use them every year, for a long period of time.

This principle can also be applied outside the sphere of business with nearly no modification. Since my own thinking is close to this, perhaps it was natural that one general magazine remarked, "Happy Science is weak because it does not have any pricey products." It went on to compare us to C Mate[*] with very expensive products, praising such operators. However, right now that group is pretty much on the brink of collapsing.

The reason why our organization has grown so large is that, from the beginning, I believed that if we asked each individual to contribute too much, he or she would not continue to believe. The reason that other groups cannot grow is that their style is to milk their limited membership for all they are worth.

This is the key point. You must realize that the same methods used in a corporation can be applied to religions. In order to grow large, you have to try to attract the greatest possible number of users or consumers. For that reason, you have to offer good things at prices that are not too much for people to afford while continuing to offer them new things. For example, for something that Happy Science may ask

---

[*] The author is referring to Cosmo Mate, a new religious movement founded in Japan in 1984 that later changed its name to World Mate.

10,000 yen for, other religious groups may demand several million yen. If this situation is analyzed at a corporate level, Happy Science clearly corresponds to a large company. Another thing that is crystal clear is the fact that the use of such methods results in more believers.

The hardship of offering good things for good prices is worth enduring. The same holds true for a company. If you discover something new, in the beginning, you should enjoy very healthy profits. But once a lot of competitive products begin to flood the market, prices will gradually slide. If you don't think that far ahead, the situation is likely to become very punishing.

Look at cars. There are many similar-looking cars. Consequently, I don't believe that you can continue for too long if you have a complacent way of thinking.

11

Using Your Own Capital— Concept of "Dam Management"

Using your own money as initial capital

My eleventh point concerns what I would call "using your own capital." When establishing a business, most people immediately think about borrowing money from a bank. For example, founders of a magazine will generally think about borrowing money and producing surplus in about three years. However, I feel that is a mediocre way of thinking. The reality is, many such start-ups find that they cannot produce a surplus in three years. They end up going belly up.

When we first started out, we faced similar conditions in terms of business administration, but we were determined to rely solely on the money we had at hand and did not take out any loans. We were committed to borrowing nothing from outside sources, but to first of all make money on our own, and then use that as the initial capital to fund the next stage of expansion in growing bigger.

When Happy Science started out in 1986, I first wrote short discourses on a word processor to create small pamphlets and distributed them at my first lecture for some income. Then we used the income that came in from these activities to purchase various kinds of equipment and furnishings for our office, even as I went about preparing for our next lecture. We didn't incur any debt whatsoever. Our style was to save the money that we made ourselves and use that as our capital for the next activity, thereby growing bigger. And in that fashion, we did indeed grow larger and larger.

This philosophy of using your own money as the base capital to enlarge an enterprise is a very healthy way of going about things. Indeed, without that you cannot have a real entrepreneurial spirit. A person who does not understand the real value of money will immediately think in terms of borrowing a lot of money and using that to run his or her business. But after that, many of them find that they can never attain their goal of turning a profit.

This philosophy of using own capital really boils down to saying that the kind of individuals who cannot save money on their own will not prove successful in running their own business. I think it's fair to draw that conclusion.

Previously, on one occasion when I moved, I happened to stumble upon a bank savings passbook from several years earlier. This surprised me as I had forgotten that I had made such savings. When I quit the company I had been working at and went out on my own, I had about three million yen in savings. But without using it, I founded Happy Science with an initial capital of zero. So, when the passbook for this account suddenly showed up several years later, I was really surprised.

Gradually build up what is small

At the start, you might think that using money on hand to start a business is a small way of going about things. You might think that if you borrow a lot of money and throw it all into the pot, you can establish a much better business. But the fact is that there are few instances of a firm failing by starting out small and gradually becoming bigger.

In Japanese businesses, there is an old saying, "Start your business under somebody else's porch or front door eaves you have borrowed. Then, you can't fail." Many new enterprises have rented large office space right off the bat and gone under. So, the trick in business is to start small and grow big, since something small can grow larger if it goes well. If you go about things that way, you surely won't fail.

The Daiei retail chain started in this fashion. Apple Computer also started out in the founder's garage. Since the money that Bill Gates used to start Microsoft came from his winnings in poker games with friends when he was at Harvard

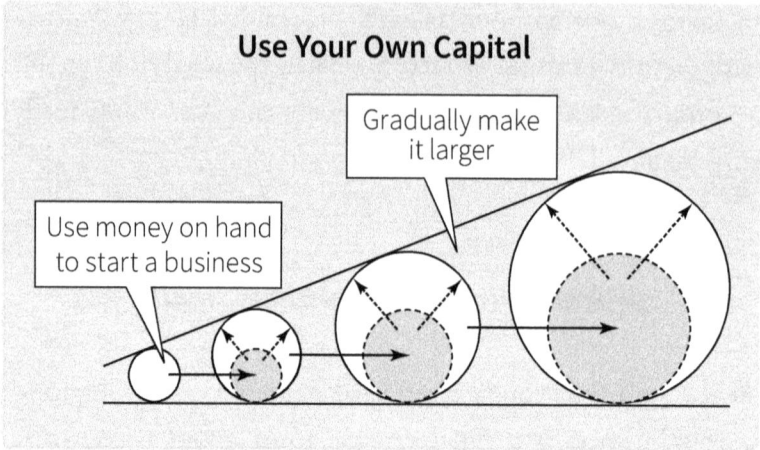

Use Your Own Capital

Gradually make it larger

Use money on hand to start a business

University, I don't know whether that qualifies as his own capital or not. But in any event, he started the company with his own funds and it has grown immense since then.

After that, the important thing is to use your money wisely while waiting for business opportunities that will enable you to grow larger. If you have that kind of money sense, you can't fail. However, people who start out by using other people's money, for example, money from a bank, money from friends, money from parents or others, is likely to fail in about a year's time. Since such people do not understand the value of money, it is easy for them to fail.

Businesses that make large investments on themselves in their initial stages are especially prone to failure and are extremely likely to fail. But individuals, who rely on the formula of first storing up their capital before growing larger at a measured pace, rarely fail.

However, to that end you have to control your desires in the beginning and really endure things. First, you have to try to make what you actually have a bit bigger. If you can do that, your business is certain to snowball and grow bigger.

In the case of Happy Science in October 1986, we first started out in this way. It was not until around August 1987 that I drew my first paycheck. I didn't want to burden the organization with my salary, so I went without pay for more than half a year. However, our organization burgeoned during that same period.

Suppose I had gone and rented office space and set up an organization where a lot of people were drawing salaries, right from the beginning, while I just went about giving lectures. Such a business structure would have soon collapsed if the number of people listening to my lectures did not increase or people did not return after listening to it once.

With that possibility very much in mind, I did everything possible to keep our expenses down to a bare minimum. I said to myself, "Well, we'll just give it a year or so and see how things work out." That was the attitude I had at the time. In the beginning, we started out that way. And confirming that we were indeed able to grow bigger, we developed into a true religion.

I believe that this approach is equally applicable to fields outside of religion. It is important to gradually build up what is small. People who have started up using their own capital are less likely to use the money carelessly. However, if a firm is started up with someone else's money, although sometimes the firm may succeed, in countless cases the firm failed as soon it hit a bump in the road.

Being in the red indicates wasteful use of resources

If a company makes a profit, then it is going to have to pay about 40 percent of that as corporate tax.[*] Therefore, the common perception is that paying corporate tax represents taking losses, so everything possible should be done not to pay this tax. That's the advice often given.

Among Japanese companies, if you added up all the small firms you would come up with several million of them, but roughly 70 percent of them are operating in the red. The reason why is that they detest paying corporate tax. They don't have to pay this tax if they don't turn a profit. That is all. Thus, they run up enormous expenses and run a small deficit. In that case, they do not have to pay corporate tax.

---

[*] at the time of the lecture.

However, this is reckless management. In the case of a business, the whole purpose of the venture is to make at least some profit, of course. And if doing so involves paying a certain amount of taxes, then that is proof of the company's validity to society. Businesses are run by effectively utilizing the limited resources within society—people, material, money, information and other things—so, if the result is not a profit, that means the management has failed. In effect, such a situation amounts to useless utilization of resources.

A company's employees represent a precious resource. Let's suppose 100 people are hired, but this puts the firm in the red. Based on the management theory I outlined in the Introduction, we can conclude that this approach did not yield results. If you hire 100 employees but end up running losses, this means you were not able to produce more results than the combined effort of 100 employees working separately.

Alternatively, let's say you start off with 100 million yen [one million dollars] in capital, but still end up running losses. That could well be an indication of wasteful use of limited resources. Consequently, it's better for a company like that to go under. It would be better for society if another company absorbed it and made better use of its human resources, capital and material.

If there are no places generating profits, society in general cannot develop. If there are spots generating profits, then the overall GDP [gross domestic product] will increase, the nation's tax revenues will increase and overall development can occur. However, if everyone is in the red, then society will find itself on a downward slope.

Internal reserve of profits is important

This philosophy of saving your own capital to grow or "internal reserve and saving" is a manifestation of the concept of "dam management." Konosuke Matsushita, Japan's "god of management," often spoke about dam management. He advocated a philosophy of building management dams.

The water of a river is generally always flowing, but sometimes the water completely dries up. This is why you build a dam; you store water and release it from there as needed, so that you can provide a stable source of hydroelectric power.

Management operates in the same way. Since there are booms and recessions, the business environment can change tremendously over a five- or ten-year span. Firms that only do well during the good times will find themselves quickly collapsing when the hard times arrive. Therefore, just as a dam always has water stored up behind it, you need to set aside a certain amount of capital in preparation for economic downturns.

The kind of person who by nature takes any and all money that comes in and uses it up right away is certain to end up in trouble. But we also see plenty of people who spend more than they take in. This is because their style is to trust that money will come in the future and count their chickens before they hatch. This will not do. After all, we must control our desires to some extent and develop the kind of financial posture whereby we can weather uncertain factors in the future. That is what is referred to as dam management. [Konosuke Matsushita also considered using dam management in areas other than money.]

However, since such dam management sometimes results in waste, you have to be careful in implementing it. If you are too cautious and think of only conserving your resources, you won't be able to develop your company. It's a matter of timing.

In the case of a physical dam, you can store water up to a certain level, but once you pass that point, you will have to release that water. The objective is not to keep storing up water, but to release water appropriately to produce something. As such, you have to be prepared to divert part of it to effective investment or to business-related expenses while setting aside a certain amount of capital. That kind of thinking is important, since having a philosophy that overemphasizes inventories won't do. Always keeping your warehouses full out of fear of product shortages is not an effective approach, either. Dam management does not mean keeping warehouses full of products.

Nonetheless, the thought that emphasizes forming your own capital is extremely important from the perspectives of both the individual and a corporation. Companies that use this approach usually do so because of some bitter lesson encountered in the past. For example, Toyota, at one time in the past, was on the brink of bankruptcy. At that time, it asked the Sumitomo Bank [currently the Sumitomo-Mitsui Bank] for financing, but was flatly refused by the bank. It was that bitter experience that gave rise to emphasis on self-financing.

Dam Management

- Set aside some capital for economic downturns
  (➡ debt-free management is best)
- Use a portion of it to make effective investments

Toyota ended up amassing great savings, which apparently exceeded one trillion yen [ten billion dollars] and was commonly referred to as the "Toyota Bank." Usually, starting a new bank branch requires around 2 billion or 3 billion yen of capital. But there are some small banks which will open a branch by borrowing money from Toyota, not from their own headquarters. So, ironically speaking, Toyota had reached the point where it can now lend money to banks.

The same was true with Panasonic. It underwent a bitter experience with money and has since adopted a management policy averse to debt. If you have the resolve to carry out company business without borrowing money, you will do just that. But if you don't have that resolve and instead think you can manage your company based on loans and debts, you won't be able to manage your company debt-free.

12

Top-Down Paradigm

A top-down arrangement is a system where The top management takes all responsibility

The twelfth point I would like to raise is the top-down paradigm. In Japanese societies, many decisions are made using a bottom-up paradigm. The top-down paradigm is an approach that has been widely accepted in Europe and North America, but in Japan, the bottom-up paradigm dominates.

The bottom-up paradigm is low-risk. A proposal comes from the lower positions and the head approves it and signs off on it. If the proposal fails, the lower-ranking people take the responsibility. The head does not have to accept any responsibility.

So, although important management decisions cannot be made by the lower ranks, there is a tendency to palm off that duty to subordinates. If the policies fail, the responsibility is shifted to the people below. What this amounts to is dumping responsibilities on individuals who do not have adequate business information, who are not being paid to make these tough decisions. In other words, people of lower positions are being made to perform the jobs of top managers.

Consequently, I believe this bottom-up paradigm is not always the best approach. In Japanese companies, the job of those at the top frequently is to do nothing more than sign off documents. They have it a bit too easy. In a top-down paradigm, the head accepts responsibility. In a top-down system, those who give the orders and directions have to accept responsibility. In return, those on the top always have a wealth of information available and must carry out R&D. I think these aspects need to be considered.

Happy Science has adopted a top-down format. In fact, religious bodies often are top-down in style. Top-down

Top-Down and Bottom-Up Styles

Top-down	● The head takes responsibility ● In many cases, things could be too late if the head is the one making all the decisions
Bottom-up	● The company could develop if the bottom provides information and proactive ideas ● The lower-ranking people could be made to take responsibility, not the head

arrangements are particularly common if it is a religious body with the founder present. Religious groups that do not use the top-down paradigm, if examined carefully, are usually not religious groups after all. In many situations where a religious veneer is used to camouflage other sales activities, a top-down system is not used. And there are quite a few of these sales promotions disguised as religions.

In other words, most religions without a founder or fundamental teachings are sales ventures disguised as religions. I find this to be a thorny problem as there are many such ventures. Nevertheless, any group that has a founder, has teachings, believes in Buddha or God and receives guidance from Heaven in order to lead people on earth has a top-down form.

In Japan in 1995, during the debate about reform of the Religious Corporate Bodies Law, there was much discussion about the relationship between religion and democracy. At that time, some people said religions are inherently undemocratic, but the Christian side retorted that religion was a top-down process stemming from God, so it didn't need to be democratic. Since religion is something that has been going on for a long, long time, there was no need for it necessarily to be democratic. This is an inherent characteristic of religion.

Decisions should be made
Near the scene of the action

The bottom-up style would be a problem if the head simply stamps documents that are being circulated. But if there is an upward flow of various kinds of information and proactive ideas from the people at the bottom, this style could also ensure the wholesale development of a company.

Even if we say that the heads make the decisions, in most companies information only reaches the heads after making a long, long journey through various strata. In many cases, when the time comes to make the final decisions at the head, it is already too late.

In that sense, I believe the core of the matter is to make decisions as close as possible to the scene of the action. If a company does not switch to a style in which decisions are made as close as possible to where the most information is available, it would be very easy for the company as a whole to become sick and feeble.

However, it will not do to adopt management methods associated with a style where those on top, be it the president, a department chief or a factory chief, can evade responsibility. Although it is best for decisions to be made close to the actual place involved, in many cases in Japan, the people on top have no real skill or responsibility. This style is never modern or futuristic.

After all, it is the people at the top who should make the toughest decisions and take the most responsibility. It is not at all good to have a situation where the farther up you go, the easier things become for you.

13

Personnel Policies Based on the Merit System— Giving Second Chances

Appreciating strong genes

The thirteenth point I want to discuss is personnel policies based on the merit system. This is related to the subject of innovation. At traditional organizations and corporations, usually, there are a very strict hierarchy and firmly established values in which decisions are based on. However, when developing and fostering new style businesses, the requirements change one after the next. In other words, the required abilities and the output expected at work also change.

What was lauded as a magnificent invention this year may be declared obsolete next year. The person who is called a great leader this year may not be considered so the following year. This is a phenomenon observable only at a developing company.

It does not occur at a company that is not developing. Places that are not developing are basically in a similar situation as an agricultural society or a stagnant society where capable people are brought down. For that reason, people don't want to stand out from the crowd; the emphasis is on the commonality. Such a non-developing society is usually ruled by jealousy. Anyone who dares to stand out is immediately put back in his place.

Although a stagnant society may exhibit strong equality, it also exhibits extremely strong jealousy. Those who stand out are punished mercilessly. However, if you are aiming to make progress, there will inevitably be disparities. It is extremely difficult to smooth out things in such a situation. In a society characterized by jealousy, there are going to be a lot of jealous people if you produce noticeable results, even if it is for the sake of making progress. It seems fair to say that in such a culture, progress is obstructed to a considerable extent.

It is important to have a culture where successful people are blessed. On this point, I believe that the United States is superior to Japan. In America, the success of individuals and corporations is highly appreciated. They understand that successful people emit a certain aura.

However, in Japan, the important thing is not to become successful, but rather to remain mediocre and live a life of neither being too capable nor too incapable. Furthermore, in Japan, if you want to stay in favor with your boss, it is better for you not to be a threat to him. If you show no threat to your superior that will undoubtedly please him. In that fashion, useless people can gradually work their way up the corporate ladder. Since capable people tend to be outspoken, they will come to be disliked; the useless ones will be promoted.

When the number of bosses who reward the incompetent grows, the organization will peak and start to collapse. This will inevitably happen. In the end, only the bootlickers, the lackluster and the harmless will get promoted. When that happens, the organization will be on its last legs.

In a good organization, you might say that strong genes are very much appreciated. Moreover, these strong genes strengthen the other genes. It is vital that strength be transmitted through the corporate genes in this fashion. You should not be regarding strong elements or components as disharmonious factors and expelling them from your organization. Instead of expelling the strong elements, absorb the strong elements and spread them throughout the entire body to make the other parts stronger. Then, your organization will become progress-oriented.

In that sense, I believe we need to adopt and emphasize the merit system. When I speak of an emphasis on the merit system, please don't think that I am referring to just illustrious job titles. Rather, I want to note that the job itself is the reward of one's capabilities. It is best to have a system in which various jobs flock to capable people. Work should be the reward. Fancy titles, money and so on are merely results, the lees. If you make those your only objectives, you will get different kinds of people.

It boils down to a case of good work coming to good workers. I feel it is important to look upon work as rewarding in its own right.

Providing second chances to those who have failed

As an organization evolves, so will its demands. There are instances in which individuals who are now highly regarded may not be so highly regarded next year. In some respects, that is not the fault of the individual concerned. In an organization, the demand changes and culture also changes. So, it is not that the current evaluation is wrong; it is just that the organization may require something different.

The person who is highly appreciated now may not be so highly regarded next year. The trends are constantly changing, so that is an inevitable development. However, if you put that same person in a different position, he or she may again be able to display his or her talents to the hilt. Therefore, as far as a changing society is concerned, I believe we need to develop mechanisms whereby an individual is able to recover from defeat, over and over again.

It is dangerous for an innovation-oriented organization not to allow its employees even one mistake. The reason why is because the systematic abandonment of obsolete sections will eliminate more people than nurture them. This always happens when the rate of progress is high. That is true for nearly all venture enterprises. Companies such as those that start out in garage workshops usually do not have people with advanced management skills in the early stages. As those companies become major corporations with tens of thousands of employees, they will start to recruit very capable individuals. When this happens, the companies could gradually put employees who were there from the beginning in a bind.

Such a manner of bringing in fresh blood and shaking up the staff is the correct approach. It is in fact proof that progress is taking place. If it is not happening, it indicates that the company is making no progress.

Take the case of Panasonic. Its first president was Konosuke Matsushita, an elementary school dropout. Since that was so, in the beginning, he said it was fine to hire people who had not gone beyond elementary school. Then he raised the bar to junior high school graduates. And as the company grew larger and larger, high school graduates. Finally, after the Matsushita empire had grown quite large, it was decided that the time had come to hire college graduates.

Konosuke Matsushita contended that it was best to hire people appropriate to the size of the company. For an evolving organization, it is impossible to recruit individuals of exceptional ability right off the bat. However, the type of people that an organization needs will change as it grows, so you must be very vigilant in this regard. You have to use the right people at the right time.

I understand that one man who had been a vice president at the inception of his company, a firm which managed to become a global giant in its first generation, is now just a regular employee. These kinds of things reportedly happen just about everywhere.

Personnel Policies Based on the Merit System

- Create an organization that appreciates strong genes and transmits them to other workers
- Create a system in which tasks flock to capable people
- Provide multiple chances to those who have failed

It is said that the snake that cannot shed its skin dies. In order to grow bigger, a snake has to shed its old skin. No doubt it is painful to shed the skin, but if that skin is not shed, the snake will die as it grows larger. The cicada, too, has to break out of its shell if it wants to fly. When an organization "sheds its skin," we call it innovation. Innovation is absolutely essential for the organization to grow larger.

The same is true for religions. When the number of Happy Science believers topped 10,000, it was time for a rather large-scale "skin shedding." At that time, the methods used up to that point were no longer applicable. Management approaches, personnel policies and ways of thinking—everything was out of sync with the situation. They had to be discarded. If we didn't innovate, we could not develop any further. We realized this around the time we hit 10,000 members.

I'd say that most religious groups are not able to overcome this 10,000-member threshold or that they stagnate when they reach the several thousand or several hundred-member level. I believe they are probably happy with just that. Consequently, if you think that you cannot make it past the 10,000-member level, then you should settle at that size. But if you have the determination to make progress, you will have to change your ways or methods. You should realize that the process will inevitably be painful. If the changes only involve changes among the management executives, that's not too much of a problem. However, if the situation gets out of hand, then ultimately, the organization head will need to be replaced. Then, the organization itself will fall apart.

Such things occur in businesses, too. Even if a person who established an organization has a strong luck, unless that person works very hard to keep innovating, in a company or wherever it may be, the limits to the capabilities of that person at the top will inevitably show. The only thing that person can do to avert this is to study on a constant basis.

When operating out of a small hole-in-the-wall factory, it is fine to pursue a small town factory approach of cultivating good ties with other people or manufacturing products for niche industries. However, as the company grows larger, more money will have to be spent and the people in charge will have to study how to handle money. Purchasing methods will be different. They will also be dealing with big corporations. Moreover, they will have to start bringing in superior talent, which in turn will give rise to work involving personnel management. Then, once they start doing business with overseas customers, they will have to hire people who can speak English because they will now have to do business in

English as well. Like this, they will be forced to make one change after another.

Since the company will have to adapt to such changes, there will inevitably be staff replacements. Not only that, those at the top must continue to study many things, too. Unless they do so, they will not be able to keep up with the changes.

If they cannot keep studying, company progress will come to a grinding halt; in fact, the company should stop its progress. If they don't stop its growth, the organization will collapse due to its own momentum. The leaders have to be perfectly aware of their own abilities and must be prepared to stop progress when the company reaches a certain limit. That, I believe, is one recipe for survival and success.

It is extremely important to place emphasis on the merit system, but since changes in culture can be the boon or bane of someone, it is very important to provide those who experienced failure with opportunities to bounce back, again and again.

14

The Theory of Decentralization

There are limits to the individual

The fourteenth point that I would like to discuss is the theory of decentralization. If we talk about this in terms of politics, it refers to things such as devolution of power to local levels. In corporations, this is the system of various business departments. This departmentalization system creates departments based on the products being manufactured and the department chief operates like the president of a small company.

As the scale of a company grows, no matter who the top person is, he or she can't keep an eye on everything; management has to be delegated and segmented.

However, at this time, you have to understand that the capable management personnel you need may not be available within the company itself. In the case of a developing company, usually, it frequently suffers the pain of finding out that many of the people who were with the company in the beginning cannot be trained up to par and eventually drop by the wayside, while some of the people brought in from the outside do not perform up to expectations. However, since there are limits to what any single human being can do, unfortunately, the company will not be able to grow bigger unless you decentralize authority to some extent.

In Section 4, I talked about strategies for the weak and strategies for the strong. I talked about how Napoleon's armies would always win when Napoleon himself was with them, but the area that his subordinates could cover to relay information by horse was limited. He could command operations within the area that a horse could reach in a day, say, about 200 km [124 mi]. However, areas beyond that would be outside the limits of his direct command. I noted that management in such areas fall apart.

In Section 10, in discussing the theory of "shallow, wide and long," I noted that regardless of whether a religion is good or bad, management theory-based analysis could be applied to it. The same holds true for warfare.

In looking at Adolf Hitler, for example, he would naturally have to be judged as evil if we look at him in terms of good and evil. When Konosuke Matsushita judged him in terms of management theory, Matsushita determined that his management had failed. The reason for this was that Hitler went to war with too many different countries.

After Hitler had triumphed over France and had Britain's back against the wall, he decided to fight the Soviet Union, too. That amounted to an overextension of the German lines. Germany did not have unlimited manpower to fill the ranks of its armies, of course. Furthermore, dispatching these forces to various fronts also required numerous commanders. Since there were not enough good officers trained, those in charge could not give proper commands. Even though they might have been able to fight in one place, they could not exert enough leadership when they were required to take command in various places.

As far as enemy attacks from the sea were concerned, it would have been possible to defend against that if Germany only needed to defend its own coasts. But after conquering France, the Germans were now forced to defend both the coasts of France and the coasts of Germany. They had to defend Poland, too, once they conquered that inland territory. When there were so many different places to defend, it did not matter how big of an army Hitler had.

Nevertheless, Hitler then pushed on and invaded the Soviet Union. Hitler chose the very same day as the day Napoleon suffered disastrous defeat when he invaded Russia. However, he was defeated by the Russian winter, too. As I mentioned earlier, command does not reach its destination when military lines are overextended. So, if there are no military brains on the actual field, decisions cannot be made. This leads to defeat.

Furthermore, when the Allied armies invaded Normandy in France, Hitler could not make a decision because he was asleep. The German commanding officers on the scene lacked the authority to make advanced decisions, so they were not able to put up a proper defense and, therefore, lost. Since things like this do happen, ultimately, it is vital to use the theory of decentralization.

Building organizations based on mutual assistance

It always takes time for people to become sufficiently trained. Even so, authority must be handed down; you must let your subordinates make the decisions, whether those are only 70 or 80 percent of your overall decisions. Otherwise, you will never grow as a whole.

However, when decentralization goes wrong, the situation will become like what we get with a vertically-divided government offices structure, where all are going their own separate ways. This leads to pointless work. So, even if authority is handed down, things won't work if you do not create an organization in which there is mutual aid and reinforcement. If that kind of structure is not created, you are going to end up with a lot of meaningless work in the organization.

For example, say that your organization has a division called the Education & Training Division. What would happen if it were divided up into the Education Division and the Training Division? What if the mandate is for the Education Division to solely engage in the creation of training software and for the Training Division to only run the seminars? What would happen then?

The Education Division would be done with its work once it creates training software and lecture material. Then, even if many seminar attendees arrive for an overnight stay, running the actual seminar would be the responsibility of the Training Division, which has nothing to do with the Education Division. So, you might end up with the Education Division having no work to do and the Training Division so busy that all its staff run so ragged and has to request to have the amount of staff doubled.

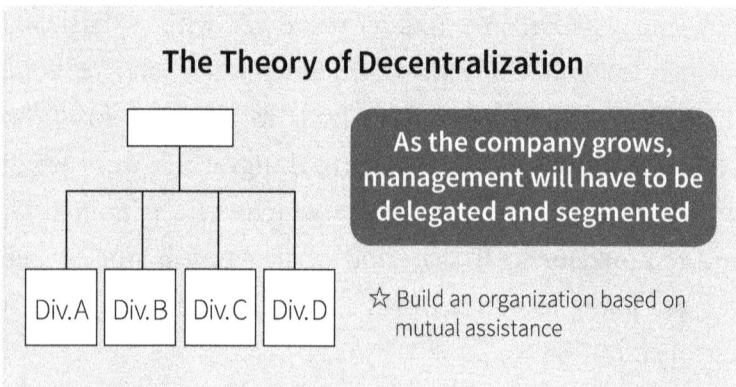

The Theory of Decentralization

| | Div. A | Div. B | Div. C | Div. D |

As the company grows, management will have to be delegated and segmented

☆ Build an organization based on mutual assistance

From a management perspective, this would all be negative. If operations were considered solely the responsibility of the Training Division, then it would become necessary to double its staff. However, the division wouldn't need those extra people all the time, but only during their busiest times. When the Training Division needs a lot of extra hands, the best approach would be to ask for help from other divisions. Decentralism easily results in these kinds of failures. Consequently, it is essential to establish systems of mutual support.

In Japan, you often hear that recruiting former officers from the Japan Self-Defense Forces [JSDF] into a company can be a mistake. That is because such individuals have a tendency to define spheres of authority too clearly. In a smaller business, if you spell things out too clearly, you will fail. The reason is that all the different sections end up doing things their own way, thereby requiring too many people to get everything done. That's the way things are in the military. This is a commonly made observation.

With decentralization, unless you have a system of mutual self-help in place, you will end up doing pointless work and efficiency of management will fall.

15

Theory of Eliminating Strata

High vertical strata can easily lead to An irresponsible system

As point number fifteen, I would like to discuss the theory of eliminating strata. When there are too many vertical strata or levels in an organization, this can lead to its demise, too. The people at the top are the very last to get necessary information, so they are unable to make proper decisions.

For example, say that 20 different individuals have to approve circulating documents. In such a case, the 17th person to receive the document is not actually making a decision on the matter. Since he will know that three more people above him will have to sign off on it, he will likely leave the decision up to them. The same process will be repeated when the 18th person gets the document, since he will believe that the 19th person is going to make the actual decision.

So, that means that the 20th person in line will make the decision. In reality though, the last person is likely to conclude that since person number 1 through 19 has already given the OK for the matter, there is nothing wrong with it. Thus, the truth is, no one is actually making a proper decision.

Consequently, you can see how too many vertical strata can easily lead to a structure lacking responsibility. However, if a matter can be decided with the approval of a single individual, then it will be clear that the person is the one who will take the responsibility.

GE [General Electric], a major company, experienced a similar sort of situation. The gloves a factory worker used on the job became worn-out, so he had to get a new set of gloves. However, at GE there was a system in place whereby such a worker could not receive his new gloves unless a request form was filled out and three supervisors signed off on it.

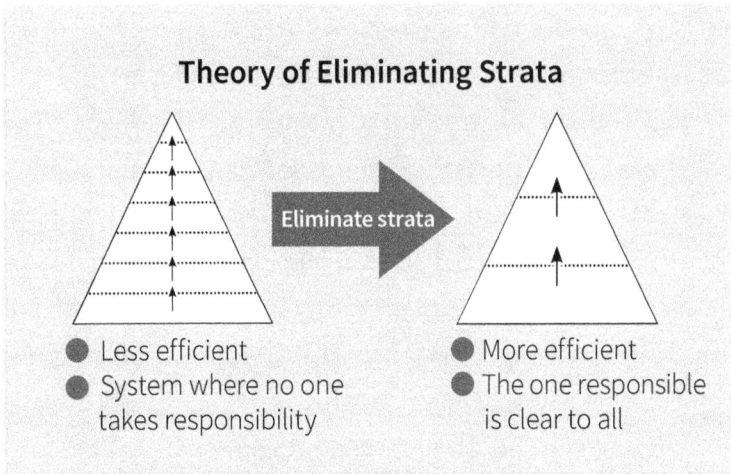

Theory of Eliminating Strata

Eliminate strata

- Less efficient
- System where no one takes responsibility

- More efficient
- The one responsible is clear to all

In such a case, the machinery had to be stopped, so that the worker could go through all the necessary procedures to get a new pair of gloves.

When this situation was pointed out to GE's president, he wondered why things had to be that way. After some investigation, apparently there was a case where a box with a dozen gloves went missing. Therefore, in order to prevent further losses, anyone wanting new gloves would have to fill out a request form.

This resulted in tremendous nonsense. Not only was the effort involved in authorizing the new gloves meaningless, there was also waste stemming from the stoppage of work operations. As for what the people at GE did, they simply stationed a box of new gloves close to where the employees were working. This case may seem ridiculous, but when organizations become super-sized, there will surely be many things that contribute to a decline in work efficiency.

This is especially true at government offices. Whenever a problem occurs, there is an alarming tendency for the number of "supervisors" to increase. Since there is such a tendency, when you get an extended vertical ladder of numerous people who have to give approval, it becomes absolutely essential to prune these ranks now and then. If you don't eliminate some of these strata, you will get a situation where work cannot proceed unless a certain person is present.

The trend to eliminate
Mid-level management positions

You want to have as few strata as possible. It is necessary to create organizations with as few strata as possible. For the past 10 years, especially at larger organizations, there has been an extremely active movement to "flatten out" organizations. Organizations are unable to survive without doing so.

To that end, there has been a movement to eliminate and wipe out mid-level management positions. Bill Gates, for instance, has said, "When the use of e-mail started, that sounded the death knell for mid-management positions." He, too, made extensive use of e-mails.

Through a local area network within a company, e-mails can directly link everyone from top management to the person in charge of a particular task and can get direct answers. So, instead of meeting face-to-face in a conference room, these parties interact through a type of written conversation. The superior can thus send a query to the person in charge of some task and get a reply back by e-mail.

With the way things are now, intermediary managers can no longer survive. Bill Gates predicted the demise of mid-level management jobs and warned people to be aware of that trend. He attributed it squarely to the advent of e-mail.

In addition, even though they have not had quite that

effect, other electronic devices such as faxes and telephones have had an impact, too. In the end, obsolete sections in companies, which existed only because management had overlooked its existence, will gradually die out along with further progress with these electronic devices.

In the case of the direct disciples of Buddha, those who could memorize and reproduce the contents of Buddha's sermon, basically those who can act as human tape recorders, would be able to make a living off of that. At the present, however, with the advent of CDs and DVDs, people could no longer live with that capability alone; more advanced skills are in demand. Now, such people would have to be able to provide excellent interpretations of the sermons in order to make a living. Now that everyone is able to listen to a lecture, different skills are in demand than those in the past.

Therefore, things have become more difficult for those providing the service. Things have become so much more convenient, so in this age, it is now very difficult to live off commissions only.

16

Theory of Restructuring— Boldly Dispose of Your Work

The sixteenth point I wish to make concerns the theory of restructuring—boldly dispose of your work. Work tends to become more diversified as an organization grows bigger. Tasks that were created a long time before will remain while new tasks are created. Furthermore, new sections will have to be created in order to regulate the various sections. That, too, will begin to create new work. Work increases in this way.

Looking at the situation at government offices, starting with those of the central government, Tokyo Metropolitan Government and Tokyo ward offices, you may wonder whether all those bureaucratic jobs are truly needed. Perhaps we may not need them. All the work having to do with Tokyo now handled by the central government could be entrusted to the Tokyo Metropolitan Government. That would be fine. And if the ward offices could do their work very efficiently, then you wouldn't even need the metropolitan government. That is the truth.

Work tends to become redundant; work is created for the sake of doing particular work. So, in trying to come up with ways to reduce costs, the most important thing isn't to cut expenses, but to think whether or not a given task is actually necessary to begin with and get rid of it if it's pointless. The immense costs come from unnecessary work.

When profit decreases, you inevitably hear various things such as, "We must bring down costs," but in many cases, there is meaningless work being done. Although no doubt such tasks were essential in the past, currently it does not matter whether or not they are done away with. The example I gave of having to get a series of approvals just to replace a pair of gloves is definitely a case of meaningless work. The greatest cost cutting is achieved by eliminating such useless tasks.

Theory of Restructuring

● Think whether or not a task is necessary to begin with and get rid of it if it's pointless

● If your work is not something that should be done by someone receiving your level of salary, you must pass that work on to someone else at a lower pay grade

● After that, do higher value-added work, more productive work or R&D

This is related to innovation. Organizations undergoing growth will find themselves in trouble if they do not constantly do this. They have to reevaluate their work and boldly abandon what is no longer needed. Getting rid of all that dead wood is fine because you will find it impossible to eliminate a job if it is actually needed. But that which can be gotten rid of should be done away with.

For instance, in Japan, postal services have been privatized. It was fine for the public sector to let go of such services. Postal services could be done by the private sector. However, certain interests did all they could to stop it from getting privatized. They went all out to keep a lid on things, so that private delivery firms like Kuroneko Yamato [Yamato Transport Co.] could not enter this business industry. In this way, the central government can reduce its deficit by giving up what can be given up.

The same holds true at a private company. The most important thing is to get rid of tasks that do not need to be done. However, some employees are certain to worry that if their tasks are done away with, they won't have any work to do and will be in jeopardy of losing their job. They will fear that they will be fired, so they cannot get rid of meaningless work. Nevertheless, you should boldly dispose of work that does not need to be done.

In that case, you must look for new work. You must create work that is more highly productive and with higher value added. If the work that you are currently doing is not something that should be performed by someone receiving your salary, you must pass that work on to someone at a lower pay grade.

When you do this, you may find that you do not have any work to perform, but if you just spend your time fooling around, you will end up being fired. Instead, your next move must be to perform work that has higher value added, has higher productivity or is R&D. In this fashion, you must strive to make yourself constantly free of your current work.

17

Steadiness and Boldness [Conclusion]

My point number seventeen has to do with steadiness and boldness. This is the conclusion on this topic of management theory. If you look at the management theory on which our organization operates, you will likely discover areas where we boldly challenge things. That is not just to be showy. We are meticulous in areas we should be meticulous and extremely steady when we need to be steady.

There are many organizations that have mimicked our ways and failed. They fail because they only look at our

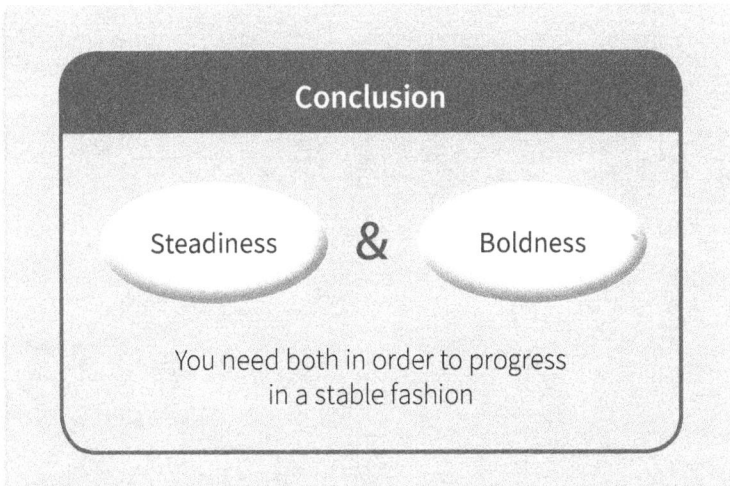

Conclusion

Steadiness & Boldness

You need both in order to progress
in a stable fashion

promotional or marketing activities and judge the whole from those things. But in truth, we are extremely prudent in the parts we are protective of.

Organizations that lack steadiness eventually go bust. On the contrary, if you are solely steady in your work, you will never grow. In the end, you have to think about being both steady and bold. While boldly seeking to win, you certainly don't want to get involved in a project where you could lose everything in one go. When getting involved in a big project, you need to aim for big results, but also need to avoid doing anything that could destroy your entire business. While doing so, you must secure and preserve what you need in order to survive.

Some people can only see the boldness of Happy Science, but we have both steadiness and boldness running in our organization. Therefore, people who have acquired Happy Science-style management skill will surely be capable of doing things with both steadiness and boldness. This is the way to make progress while doing work in a stable fashion.

Chapter Two

Management Tips:
The Wisdom to Survive Deflation

Lecture given on October 9, 2002

1

The Correct Way of Looking at Deflation

"Deflation is an economic downturn" is a mistaken idea

Chapter 2 is titled, "Management Tips." The title may be a little vague, but I mean to discuss things that will serve as a reference at key points in time.

What I would particularly like to write about now is how to look at deflation. Lately, we often hear the word *deflation* and that we are now in an era of deflation. Many people are discussing what the best way is to respond to deflation. They are afraid that deflation means an economic downturn.

Simply put, deflation is the drop in the price of goods. The price falls and, even worse, salaries also drop. Under the current deflation, even the salaries of civil servants are being cut back. Now, many people believe that wage cuts equate to economic downturn. The mass media are definitely echoing this sentiment.

I would like to point out, though, that this idea has a flaw. Indeed, deflation is accompanied by cuts in pay across the board as well as a drop in the price of goods. Many people believe that manufacturers and retailers who make money when goods are selling at a higher price suffer from price drops. Not only that but they also believe that, since the salaries of civil servants are reduced, the purchasing power of the population as a whole weakens, too. This is why they think deflation naturally results in an economic downturn.

However, this is a mistaken idea. "Price of goods falls during deflation"—this means that the basic level of economy shifts downward. In other words, the range of economic activity expands.

For example, people who were previously unable to

Deflation is Not Always an Economic Downturn

Price of goods falls during deflation

⬇

Things previously unaffordable are now affordable

⬇

A chance for increase in consumption and revenue

purchase expensive goods on account of their low salaries will begin to buy those very goods as they become less expensive. Services that were once too expensive for an ordinary person will become obtainable once the prices are reduced. This means people can buy goods because they are cheaper. It is a concept that is very easy to understand.

If a car that costs 2 million yen [20 thousand dollars] is reduced to 1.5 million yen or 1 million yen, people who could not previously afford the car can now buy it. People who just could not find the leeway to spend 2 million yen on a car will be able to buy that car if its price drops to 1.5 million, 1 million or 900,000 yen.

Thus, people who had no chance of buying certain goods will be able to purchase those goods now that their prices have fallen. If people are now able to buy that car for 1 million yen that they could not before afford when it cost 2 million yen, sales will rise to compensate for that 50 percent cut in the sales price. This is how things should be under deflation.

This is not an economic contraction, but rather an economic expansion. Under deflation, if a company sets out to sell the same number of cars it was selling before, it will suffer a 50 percent cut in sales when the car is reduced in price from 2 million to 1 million yen. On the contrary, if the company is mindful of the fact that it will gain new customers as a result of the price drop, it may very well see an increase in sales. That is, the company will be able to expand its scale of economy. The company will suffer in sales if it fails to take action, but will improve sales if it works hard to take advantage of the change in circumstances.

Furthermore, many services only targeted people with high income. Services excluded individuals if they made anything less than 8 million yen [80 thousand dollars] a year, if their salary was not at least 10 million yen or if they did not make at least 20 million yen a year. These services have become cheaper, though, allowing individuals of lower social strata to take advantage of them.

High-class gyms and other such establishments that suffer a decline in customers will naturally have to cut prices. Membership fees at golf clubs, which used to cost an arm and a leg, have become cheaper. Now, people who are lower down on the company food chain will be able to join those clubs. Many places where only the upper management and managers of top companies could afford to go are now accessible to the average workers. This results in more people being able to afford such things. If high-class tennis clubs lower their fees, the average person will be able to start playing tennis there.

Also, as a result of deflation, many hotels no longer strive to be as luxurious as they were before. They now have no choice but to lower prices for accommodations and offer lunch buffets and other services to bring in customers. This allows lower income individuals to dine at expensive hotels where they could not previously afford to eat. We must remember that deflation will result in an economic downturn only if we stand idly by and make no effort to improve the situation. Therefore, it is a mistake to believe that deflation immediately results in poor economic conditions.

People invariably believe that economy should be steadily growing at the current pace. Over the postwar decades, they have come to expect and grown accustomed to the idea that if this year is 100, then next year will be 102, 103 or 105 and that salaries and sales will increase each year.

Now that everything is going down, however, they're shocked. People talk of how tough the economic landscape is because of deflation, but that view is mistaken.

The deflationary trend will not stop

Some people say, "Since deflation is tough, we must come up with countermeasures." Various politicians, as well as the world of finances, are urging the government to take various means to bring the economy toward inflation again and the government is seeking ways to combat the situation.

However, this is a trend, so it will not stop. Why won't it stop? I will tell you exactly why. Symbolic of the factors contributing to deflation is the retail company, Uniqlo. Its products are popular now, although they may not seem so high-quality. Uniqlo sells many casual clothes such as t-shirts with simple and plain designs. To add, Uniqlo products are more than affordable.

The reason to this is that Uniqlo products are manufactured in China. Various textiles are produced under rigorous conditions to match the quality of the corresponding goods made in Japan. However, since labor fees are low in China, cost prices are significantly reduced.

Uniqlo's rapid growth has contributed to the demise of other retailers such as Daiei. The products are so cheap that many other retailers have been defeated despite lowering prices of their own. Uniqlo sells many of its goods from around 1,000 yen [10 dollars]. Normally, retailers cannot gain profit by selling clothes at such a cheap price, but this has really caught on.

Uniqlo is one symbol. What I really want to say is that one of the reasons for deflation is Chinese production—going to China to produce goods on a par with the quality of Japanese goods. China's metropolitan areas are going through major development, but even so, office workers in these areas still only make about 20,000 or 30,000 yen [200 or 300 dollars] a month. Factory workers in the metropolitan areas only make about 10,000 yen a month.

Fighting this trend is quite tough. These labor costs are roughly equivalent to what Japanese people were making in the 1940s and 1950s. At these low labor costs, you would be able to sell goods in Japan for much lower prices if you could make them as good as those produced in Japan.

Salaries in metropolitan areas may be low, but they are even lower in the rural areas. Countless farmers live only on tens of thousands of yen a year. This is nearly a life of self-sufficiency.

Roughly 700 million people live at this level in the rural areas of China, whereas approximately 600 million people live in the metropolitan areas [statistics according to the Chinese National Statistics Bureau Report for 2008].

Although the standard of living in China's most advanced metropolitan areas is nearing that of Japan's standards today, China is, on the average, decades behind Japan. In the countryside, many people have the same standard of living and wages as we had in Japan before WWII. Giving these people the necessary technology, allowing them to produce goods on the same level as those made in Japan, will naturally result in lower prices when the goods are sold in Japan. This is why so many Japanese manufacturers have begun transferring production to China.

The same thing is happening in India. India has a population of 1.2 billion people and China has a population of 1.3 billion people. At present, India and China are continuing to grow stronger industrially as markets are becoming liberalized.

Japanese companies simply cannot compete with countries that are making the same goods and paying salaries equivalent to what the Japanese people were getting in the late 1940s, 1950s and 1960s. The companies making the same level of products as their counterparts in China or India will inevitably go out of business. This is why some sectors of the economy appear to be very weak right now.

What would happen if China and India, having a total population of over 2 billion between them, experience a strong economic boom as Japan did 30 or 40 years ago? Since the world is interlinked through trade, there will most certainly be a drop in the price of goods.

Japanese agricultural products are expensive, too. Japanese people say they are afraid of pesticides used in foreign agricultural products and that there are pesticides in spinach from China; they are always saying how scared they are of foreign produce. If Japanese people are afraid of pesticides, foreign countries will stop using them, too.

Thailand, for example, has gradually come to create produce that are in line with Japanese preferences. In this way, things will gradually be produced overseas. Wages are low in these countries; they are gradually rising, but there are still decades of a gap between these countries and Japan. For this reason, produce from these countries with lower wages are bound to be cheaper unless high duties are imposed upon them. Japanese produce will not be able to put up a competition.

There is nothing mysterious about this phenomenon. Over 20 years ago when I lived in the U.S., hardly any clothes or toys had "Made in the USA" on them. "Made in Japan" was also on the way out during that period. Many goods would have "Made in Taiwan" or some other country on them.

It was very strange that the U.S. had become a nation that mostly sold goods made in other countries. At that time, goods sold in Japan were still being made in Japan, including clothes and all other types of goods. In the U.S., though, most goods were no longer made in America; they were manufactured in Asia and other regions.

I believe Japan is moving in the same direction, gradually becoming more and more like the United States. Japan has the purchasing power that comes with being a developed country, so we are now entering an era in which we are buying up large amounts of goods from countries that are making cheaper goods.

You can no longer deliberately increase the price of items that have become cheap in order to protect Japanese products. It is no longer possible to say, "Keep buying Japanese products" and keep prices high within Japan. We have entered an era where we must buy huge quantities of goods from those that sell at cheaper prices. The same thing that happened to the U.S. is happening in Japan now. Therefore, it is absolute that prices are going to fall. There's no way of halting the deflationary trend. However, it's a mistake to think that deflation will cause an economic downturn. As I mentioned in the beginning, deflation causes the basic level of economy to fall. Then, the people in the lower income brackets are able to grab a slice of the life that was enjoyed by the people who were previously in the upper and middle strata of society. Deflation expands the possibilities for that class.

As a result, even though we cannot halt the deflationary trend, it is a mistake to think that deflation equates to an economic downturn.

A change in mindset can lead to infinite possibilities

If deflation occurs, the price of land as well as the construction costs will steadily decrease. Furthermore, bank loan interests will also fall, although banks nowadays seldom offer loans. If the prices of land decrease, construction costs fall and the interest on bank loans drop, then it will be no surprise at all if the economy hits a good stretch. It's not at all strange for the economy to improve, with many buildings rapidly built.

However, the economy is not picking up because people do not understand this. They are repeatedly saying, "We're heading for recession." They must think about how the era in which we live is going to unfold by looking at the macroeconomic trend or the overall trend.

Looking at this from a wider perspective, you would see that since the costs of buildings fall, an era will come when people who previously never considered building a new house would consider building one. If a house is getting old, people would consider rebuilding it. People who do not own land, who live in flats and apartments, will be able to have their own homes. Deflation will herald that kind of era.

So, it does not mean there are no opportunities left. There is a great deal of business opportunities. The bright spots from the perspective of management are to be found in a wide variety of areas. Frankly speaking, tragedy lies in what is between the managers' ears. This is tragic, so the situation is helpless. Keep the status quo and your business will dwindle. Change your frame of mind and you will see infinite possibilities.

2

Prosperity during Deflation

Working hard and diligently

What must be done in an era of deflation? If I were to describe the era of deflation in a slightly more intuitive way, it is a trip back to the past. It is as if you were caught in a time warp and have gone 20 or 30 years back in time. It is important to get a good sense of the lifestyle back then, since we are going back to that era.

Once you have grasped that sense, what should you do? What you have to know is, "It will no longer be possible to get a high-level income by simply taking it easy. It won't be possible to achieve big-figure revenues by selling high-priced items and cruising along." This is surely so.

In other words, "going back to the old days" means we have to work harder and more diligently than we have been doing. Such times will come. Days when one could make a lot of money, simply by working the numbers, all the while taking it easy and just breezing along—that era is over. That's what it means. No one is going to be able to just whip up business that way, by taking commission in return for adding a little bit of service or by just pushing around a few numbers. That sort of thing will naturally be weeded out as time goes on. Instead, the trend will be to work hard and diligently. Otherwise, there can be no such thing as prosperity during deflation.

A few years back, the DVD version of the animation, *Kyojin no Hoshi* [Star of the Giants]* came out on sale. Kyojin no Hoshi is an animation that ran when I was a boy. In those days, it was so popular that people used to say that all the bathhouses were left empty when this animation was on. This kind of very old animation was brought back and sold on DVD. The trend now is to go back to the old days.

We live in an era when a path is opened through tenacity, diligence, passion and effort. This is the way to combat the era of deflation. We have to go back a bit to doing things like how people used to do in the past. It simply won't be possible to take it easy and make a lot of money at the same time. Also, people won't be able to do business by just taking commission or lending out their name and reaping the profits. Those things are finished. Having real substance is the critical factor; the kind of business that works with real substance will always be around. Please put in a little more effort. Please stop thinking that you can make a living without raising a sweat.

---

* A Japanese baseball *manga* [comic] that was serialized in 1966. A TV animation also aired starting in 1968. The protagonist attains success through sheer determination and effort. Many sports manga followed this style.

Businesses trying to make impressions or just for show will disappear, since they have no substance. Whatever you do, it will have to have real substance. "There is substance here. We address a real need. We work hard, because people need what we have to offer"—businesses with such thoughts will thrive.

On the other hand, the kind of business where the value of the apartment goes up without you having to do anything, where all you had to do to make money was to just resell it for a profit—that kind of business will not be possible. Making money just from trading stocks will be a bit tough. Such kind of things will gradually get more and more difficult to do.

Businesses with substance will have possibilities. You just have to make efforts to work at them diligently. Automakers, for instance, are going to have to manufacture cars for 1.5 million yen that they are currently making for 2 million yen. If their competitors start turning out cars for less than 1.5 million yen, they will have to undercut that even more and make cars for 1 million yen. And this is the effort you will be required to put in.

Then, how could you make this possible? The only way forward for those who can't offer a single word of wisdom is, simply put, for them to work harder. They will have to raise a sweat and work a bit more, though this may be against the trend.

Even if you had been taking it easy working as an automaker with a two-day weekend, you will have to work on Saturdays, too, once the company is on the verge of bankruptcy. We're in an era where you have to refuse overtime pay, even if you do work overtime. Unless you do so, the price of cars will not drop; you will not be able to get ahead of China and India.

Therefore, we must "go back to the old days." If you are someone without much wisdom, you must work longer hours—from 8 hours to 10 hours or from 10 hours to 12 hours—in order to open the way to the future. Companies where people still work 8-hours a day and take it easy will go bust, but those where the workers switch to working 10 hours a day and make an effort to put in those extra 2 hours will not go bust. Furthermore, they will increase their share of the market by as much as the companies that do go bankrupt.

In this way, it's a bit like going back in time. You will not have a future unless you give up your easy ways. This strategy does not use wisdom.

Cutting waste and reducing overall cost

Now, what would your options be if you had a bit more wisdom? First, you must apply your wisdom to reducing costs. This must be implemented thoroughly.

Up until now, in a growing economy, parts manufacturers and everything else could expect growth everywhere; nonetheless, now it is necessary to reconsider costs. Aside from parts, various other cost components must be checked without exception. As I have just stated, this has to be done very thoroughly.

Even Panasonic [formerly Matsushita Electric Co., Ltd.], a gigantic company, underwent a massive reform. Previously, Panasonic had been using a department system, where every business unit of the company had operated independently. This was good for growth, but there was also a lot of waste. As part of the same company, many in-house divisions could offer assistance to each other, such as sharing common items. However, with the departments operating independently, this was not always possible, which led to waste.

Panasonic therefore restructured itself by removing the walls between the departments. Although all Panasonic departments were aware of their inefficiencies from before, they did not do anything about it due to good economic conditions. However, they began to realize that something must be done.

Usually, sections within the same company could share items that are purchased externally. However because they were divided into different departments, they would not work beyond their own wall. They were inefficient.

In addition, there were also inefficiencies in the department system itself. This is because they were able to make unnecessary positions at will. Each department could have similar positions, allowing redundancies to exist when seen as a whole. Due to these reasons, Panasonic smashed the department system that had worked well for them during their period of development.

In order to reduce costs, superfluous personnel must be cut and waste of resources and raw materials, etc. must be minimized. Moreover, waste in sales channels that are separately operated by individual departments must be cut.

Panasonic has now implemented "federal management" and has many subsidiaries. Nevertheless, some of the subsidiaries did not follow the parent company but stuck to their own opinions and did not cooperate very well with each other. So, they had to be brought together into a common direction and be made easier for opinions to be raised and heard.

In such a way, waste within the system, waste of personnel, waste of resources and raw materials, and waste of sales, or essentially the waste of energy, must be reduced. There is waste in terms of products, too, of course.

What will happen if waste is reduced? Naturally, cost price will come down. This is a matter of course. Cost price will drop and you can make your goods much more cheaply, enabling you to beat your competitors. We must consider how to reduce costs across the board in this way.

The most primitive method for coping in an era of deflation is, as previously mentioned, to extend working hours. If you intend to do something without planning anything specifically, then first of all, you should start with this. If you were to use more wisdom, the next thing will be to think of a way to reduce organizational costs and minimize expenses. There is waste that was created during the development period, so it is necessary to reduce this waste.

All companies have waste. Perhaps it is better to refer to this as having faults rather than having waste, as every company has its faults. Everyone could overlook some of the faults when conditions are good, but not so when the company is losing to its competitors. Therefore, it is extremely important to find your faults and correct them.

Institutions that worked under the assurance of the state's safety net and that had been certain that it would never fail are all at risk now. It is risky for you to think you will not go under. On the other hand, you could think of many things that need to be done if you think you are in danger.

Let's take a look at the things taken for granted since you've grown and stayed profitable so far. If you think, "What would we do if we were going under?" you will find unnecessary areas that you can cut. Those are the areas you must cut.

A balance that is in the black now may go into the red later on, requiring you to consider what you'd stop doing if you began losing money. "We're making 100 million yen in profit now, but let's suppose things break even in three years and turn into a loss after that. If so, what will we stop doing?" This is what you need to think about right now. One way to respond to this is to cut out what is wasteful now and avoid going into the red. You need to shave off the wasteful parts within the permanent and systematic things.

Creating sections with high added value

Once you save some money, you should invest it in sections that are highly likely to grow in the future. How much and when you make this investment are important factors of competition among companies. After all, the company that's quicker to invest in areas with high potential is the one that will win, five or ten years down the road.

You will go under if you fail to invest because you're in the red. You will surely lose, as others around you will keep making better and better things. You need to stop wasteful drains on your money and return to profitability, set aside money, invest that money in areas of potential and win the competition.

The first stage of wisdom comes from the need to examine ways to systematically cut down the cost. As I mentioned before, countries like China and India that have low labor costs become very competitive. In the future, prices will surely drop, so the second stage of wisdom will be to create sections with high added value. This will be the next survival plan.

You cannot keep producing things that can also be produced elsewhere. You should not expect that product to exist on your lineup 10 years later. Japanese companies will not be able to survive on their current products the moment the countries playing catch-up become capable of producing those products.

So, the only thing that will allow you to survive will be nothing other than to increase your added value one level higher. Things accomplished with more research, more advanced technologies and more wisdom—these are the things that will make the countries trying to catch up to Japan take more time in order to do so. If you do not make further progress, it is like saying, "I'm just going to sit and wait for my death."

Therefore, it is important to improve technology, to increase the quality of content, and to make products with higher added value that will not let others catch up with you. For that purpose, you need to invest in education and you need time to undertake research.

Three things that must be done

As I have already mentioned, the first thing that needs to be done in an era of deflation is to increase your hours working hard.

Be aware, though, that there are times when a salesperson returns to office after drinking coffee at a cafe and compiles a false report saying, "I visited Company X." Simply increasing the number of working hours would be meaningless. The content is important, too.

A salesperson's schedule could state that he visited Company X, but if he actually went to a movie theater because it was raining and then returned to the office, this would be a waste of an eight-hour working day. You must check the content of this wasted eight-hour working day. Many people go to the movie theater or a cafe and wonder to themselves, "How can I kill time until 5 o'clock?" Trying to get people like this to work hard during work hours is an important job, too.

How to Survive During Deflation

- Work hard and diligently
- Cut waste and reduce costs
- Create sections with high added value

There are many slackers in factories as well. There are also companies that halt operations whenever a problem arises. Some companies work well doing this, but if a not-so-good company tries to emulate this approach, it will only end up with workers taking it easy and saying, "There was a problem in some section" as if it weren't their business. This happens frequently.

Major automakers like Toyota perform good quality control. When a problem occurs somewhere in their factory, they stop the machinery and assembly lines and do an immediate check to prevent producing defects.

What would happen if a third-rate company tries to copy this? Everyone would stop their work, gather around and hold meetings here and there, one after another. But you cannot efficiently make products by doing such things. Therefore, just because a company operates well under such form of quality control does not mean this applies to all.

I have already talked about increasing working hours. If I were to go a step further, this would mean improving the content of hours spent at work. You must thoroughly inspect how much time is being wasted at work and how much waste the content of work contains. It boils down to an inspection of waste in the time and the content relating to work.

The second approach is to reassess costs across the board. You must fight to lower costs.

The third approach is not to be passive when it comes to sections with high added value, such as R&D.

In essence, this is what it means: "You cannot survive unless you create something that others cannot imitate. It does not matter how small or minor a section is; if possible, you must try to make a section which is and will continue to be number one in your country. If not, the company may disappear in five or ten years. Something that can be replaced by another or a product other companies can copy is highly likely to be eliminated."

3

A Time When
Wisdom Is to Be Refined Further

Problems with the work done
At Japan's banks and public offices

In trade, bankruptcy of a company does not cause problems for buyers because another company can easily cover for that. However, from a seller's perspective, this can be harsh and unforgiving. Even if one trading company goes bankrupt, others will just increase their trade instead.

The same goes for manufacturers. Even if one auto company goes bankrupt, things will be fine because many other auto companies would work harder.

This goes for banks, too. A bank could close down without causing serious repercussions. This has been so since some time ago.

Nearly 10 years ago, I said, "In Japan, there are more than 20 times the necessary number of banks. If they are not weeded out to some degree, they would not be able to serve the people of Japan." Things have happened as I predicted [see *Hanei-no-Ho* (The Laws of Prosperity), IRH

Press, Chapter 4 'Successful Thinking']. Japanese banks were gradually pressured to do so; now, city banks have been reorganized into the Three Megabanks.

This is something everyone has been feeling since a while ago. There is not much added value in the work that Japanese banks do. This is because there were two types of public offices in Japan. The first type was the civil servants, in other words, the state and local government employees. The second type was the bank. The bank was a "public office," too.

All banks were completely supervised by the government, so they were only able to produce a similar level of service. This was a remnant of the rationing system, a state very similar to the times during the wartime regulations of 1935-45 [Showa period, Years 10-20]. Bank employees could not work freely at all. They observed the government regulations. In addition, proposals submitted to them by companies had to be decided upon and approved by circulating internal memos. This is no different from how a public office runs.

When I used to work at a trading company, there was a time when I associated with a major bank that was rumored to have risky management. It ran almost exactly like a public office. The bank would respond to a proposal about a year after its submittal. The reply to a proposal I submitted to a bank branch one summer came a year later, in the summer of the following year. What was the bank's reply? "We have now circulated this to our head office."

In short, they were playing for time. With regard to proposals, banks generally play for time to avoid doing any work, since there are so many matters that are disadvantageous to them. Since corporate negotiations are matters where companies try to take the upper hand, ultimately, banks are put at a disadvantage. Thus, for banks, the longer they take to handle corporate proposals, the better it is. This is because they believe it is beneficial for them to stay firm, put the companies on hold and shelve the proposals.

The same goes for public offices. Their basic pattern is, "Do not do anything unless the customer repeatedly asks for it." Public offices have recently sped up their processes across the board a little, but basically, the longer customers are put on hold, the more advantageous it is for the offices. Banks are the same. The average individual customer might be different, but the person in charge of corporate negotiations usually asks the banks to lower the interest rate on loans a little or to further decrease the amount of deposit.

Regardless of the fact that compensating balances are prohibited, in practice, Japanese banks have forced companies to do this. They have allowed companies to borrow 1 billion yen, but made them leave 300 million yen in the account as a fixed-term deposit. This is the same as just loaning 700 million yen. Banks lend companies 1 billion yen, but they tell those companies to leave 300 million yen as deposit.

It is a complete waste of effort for companies doing business with banks like these to negotiate with the banks about cancelling the 300 million yen deposit and lowering the deposit amount. It is a total waste of time. Banks are just going to sit around and do nothing.

Usually, you should be able to use 1 billion yen if the bank lends you 1 billion yen. But the bank may tell you to leave 300 million yen as deposit. If you look weak, the bank may tell you to leave the entire 1 billion yen as deposit. When the economy was good, banks used to tell companies, "If you leave 1 billion yen as deposit at the bank for about a month, you can use 700 million yen later." This is where banks are being attacked now. Their work did not add much value and their work were no different from that of public offices. This is why banks are currently under attack.

The point is, they are under attack because they slowed down their business pace. Public offices as well as banks have been subject to steady organizational disruption. They have come under attack because their way of work slowed the development of capitalist society and market economy. Banks are being told, "You don't call that work."

Furthermore, banks are less likely to lend money to people who want to start a new business because they cannot trust such people. Banks don't make any effort. Banks keep lending money to companies that have existed for decades, but are unwilling to lend money to people who want to start up a new business because they are scared to take on the responsibility. They don't lend money because they are afraid that the new company might fail. Similar businesses are under attack and experiencing a downturn.

Engage in serious reflection and Make much more effort

Businesses like these must experience hard times. If they do not experience hardships, they will not be able to produce something good. They should experience many, many hardships. That would be good for the world, for the people, and for themselves.

They did not recognize that their work was unnecessary. They did not understand enough that they have not been doing a good job. They are under attack because they received high salaries despite not doing good work. They need to do serious self-reflection on this. This is necessary, as is much, much more effort.

Banks are able to work about 10 times more than they are doing now. They must have been able to perform jobs with about 10 times more added value. They would have been able to do so if they had had the courage to take on risk, the courage to act more with their customers in mind or the courage to increase their work speed. Now, they are being asked to reflect on this.

The same story goes for general contractors. They have come under pressure due to an economic downturn in the structural industry; their oligopolistic conditions have allowed them to work only for high prices. The contractors are under pressure because they unjustly increased their prices since they were able to function as an oligopoly and even monopolized the market to a considerable extent. They would not be forgiven unless their services, including costs, improve to meet customer needs.

This trend is not simply a case where they're heading for bankruptcy and heading into a recession, but a good thing. This is not a bad thing because the market is striking back by saying, "Make more effort. Employ more wisdom. Refine your wisdom. We won't simply let you receive high salaries after lacking ingenuity for decades." Now, they must experience hardships, employ wisdom, make reforms and implement changes to do more work that is useful to the world and for the people.

There are various shops and discount stores. But if all they do is sell goods, they will have a tough time surviving because there are countless alternatives for that. It is a tough business to survive in such a situation. Therefore, you must ask yourself, "How do I survive?" Even if you were to go bankrupt, some other place would sell similar goods. If you were to talk about your low prices only, there will always be a place with even lower prices. This is why you would have a tough time.

Consequently, the only thing you could do is, never stop studying. "What do people need? What do they want or what will they want in the future?" There is no way forward, unless you do your best to think about such things and prepare products, services and so on.

Hence, you should think that, although now is a tough time, it is also the time to refine your wisdom.

4

The Fourfold Path in Management

The idea, "customers first" and Various other knowledge and wisdom

Happy Science advocates love, wisdom, self-reflection and progress as the Fourfold Path. From a different perspective, you could consider all of these as teachings for managers.

First, let's take a look at the teaching of love. This means "customers first," "for the customers" and "service first." Love is to do your job with the customers in your mind.

What is wisdom? Using manufacturing as an example, this relates to steadily creating products of high quality, developing advanced technology and discovering new knowledge. Aside from knowledge, there is wisdom that comes from it. New specialized knowledge, advanced knowledge, the know-how about making things and operating a business—these are wisdom necessary for managers.

There is no progress without reflecting on Failures and weaknesses

What is self-reflection? Since there are a lot of failures in management, you must reflect on them, one by one. It's the same for managers as it is for non-managers; those who are incompetent put all the blame on others, such as the government, a business sector, a foreign country, a new competitor and so on.

This is how companies go bust. Individuals like this fail, but so do such companies. Companies and people who fail are those who blame others and blame the environment in which they operate. If deflation occurs, deflation is to blame; if inflation occurs, inflation is to blame; if neither inflation nor deflation occur and the situation stabilizes, that is to blame—it is never their fault.

However, even under the same circumstances, one shop can prosper while another declines. There must be a reason for this. Therefore, there is no chance of progress for companies that do not engage in self-reflection.

As I mentioned earlier, every company has its own weakness. There is not a company without one. They are still alive because they have strong points that compensate for their weak points. They either have strengths that even out their weaknesses or have strengths that are greater than their weaknesses.

177

However, if you want to take it to the next level, you must reflect on your weaknesses. Executives should ask themselves what weaknesses exist within their own company. Then, the employees should carefully inspect and find what their company's weaknesses are. Moreover, they should all see their company from the perspective of the customers. They must see how the customers evaluate their company.

When your company's items are not selling well, you may think it's due to deflation, which causes a drop in the income level of the customers. However, this does not mean competitors throughout the country are experiencing a decrease in sales in the same way.

People will continue to buy things that they need, even if their income may reduce. They cannot *not* buy things. A house is necessary. So are food and clothes. People will continue to buy things that they need.

However, when people's income decreases, they will become more selective in choosing what to buy. They will stop buying things that are not good or of little value. They will go shopping to places that sell items of value and that offer better buy. That is all. If you are going to blame others, you should do it after all your competitors have gone bankrupt.

Let's say that a shop goes bankrupt. Can you say this is because of recession? There are shops growing elsewhere.

Let's say that a supermarket has gone bankrupt. You might say this is due to recession, but this is not so. It went bankrupt because other shops are making steady progress.

It is difficult to accept this. Until then, you loved your company and were complacent and boastful. You, as manager, may have felt good. This is why it is painful for you to acknowledge that your company is bad, has a flaw or has failed. Nevertheless, you cannot survive without accepting what is in front of you; you will only sit and wait for your death.

Therefore, the teaching of self-reflection is extremely important, particularly in managing a business.

Listen to the opinions of others
And make careful observations of them

The act of self-reflection is something that you, yourself, can only do. Other companies will not be so kind as to give their objective opinions. Do you think that a company would come right out and reveal the problems its competitor has? The competitor could improve if the company does reveal this, so it won't. The company is waiting quietly and happily for the competitors to die out. They are silently watching and thinking to themselves, "That company will be gone in three years. When it does, we can take its customers."

Companies generally will not give each other advice on where they can improve their management. Anyone who does is a Mr. or Ms. Nice Guy. You say it, you lose. Mr. or Ms. Nice Guy will lose.

Let's take the Asahi Breweries Company as an example. Although they were falling behind their competitors, they came out with their beer called Asahi Super Dry and regained ground. This is putting pressure on the Kirin Brewery Company and giving it serious competition. Now, they are battling it out for the top spot in the beer industry. In those days, the person who became the CEO of the Asahi Breweries was not from a beer company, but from the banking sector. The vice president of a bank was installed as the CEO of the Asahi Breweries.

His attitude was simply to visit other beer companies in a humble manner as he had absolutely no knowledge of beer. His strategy was to visit other breweries and listen to them carefully. He positioned himself as someone who needed complete guidance in all things related to beer and brewing. He listened very carefully to critical comments on his company's products and the company itself, as well as on how to make a product that would sell.

As a result, he learned an important flaw in the company's management. Asahi Breweries did not go out and recover expired products. Beer loses its flavor over time, making it taste quite bad. For that reason, the CEO of the Asahi Breweries made an essential business decision to recover all its expired beer products.

In addition, after having asked the consumers, "What kind of beer would you like?" he made sample products and observed their response. In this way, Asahi Breweries thought in its own way and sold its Super Dry. Then, the company that gave the advice lost. This is how it happens. The company that points out a competitor's weakness by being a Mr. or Ms. Nice Guy and giving the best advice, thinking that the competitor is an amateur, loses out. Now, instead of giving advice, that company finds itself seeking advice. It must go and ask why it lost. This is something you should be really careful about. Because of this, competitors very rarely tell you how you could do better. In such situations, people generally wait for you to collapse and say nothing.

Yet, a lot can be learned through humility. This is the trick. Since managers are full of pride, they don't like to listen to the opinions or the advice of others. But as I spoke of the man who showed humility, it may be better to adopt an attitude whereby you ask for a little advice from others.

You can keep making progress by asking for advice, but only until your competitors become aware of the fact that giving you advice would pose a risk for them. When they notice that it is dangerous to give you advice, they no longer will. But until then, there are Mr. and Ms. Nice Guys who give advice to those who say, "It's tough for us too. It's hard. Could you give us a little advice? How is it that your company is able to sell so much?" If they do, that will be your chance. You will be delighted if a company tells you why it is successful while you are not.

Managers who still feel that things are not going well for them are probably aware of the limits to their own ability, so they also must listen to the opinions of others. They must listen to the opinions of their customers, of course, but they must listen to the opinions of their competitors, too.

Your competitors will not tell you why they are successful and why you are not, but there are times that they might. Furthermore, though they may not explicitly tell you, you may be able to get a feel of their hints.

People have the tendency to boast about their secrets to success. They tend to want to give some advice when they see that you are behind them. They feel compelled to give you a word when they see you as the underdog. Such times are opportunities for you. Therefore, it is necessary to ask your competitors and the people who know your business sector well. If you are having a tough time in your business, you should visit shops running a similar business to yours and observe how they run their businesses. Without such efforts, you cannot make further progress.

The Fourfold Path in Management

1. Love — Work with your customers in mind

2. Wisdom — Specialized knowledge, the know-how on business operations, etc.

3. Self-reflection — Reflect on your company's failures and weaknesses

Ex: Listen to the opinions of others, observe other companies, etc.

↓

4. Progress — Improved management and prosperous business

5

Difficult Times Are Opportunities to Change Yourself

So far, I have given various management tips. Times when everything is difficult and tough are times of opportunities. Such times are opportunities for all of you to transform. No one will transform if people are pulling in profits and enjoying a period of prosperity. The very face of adversity spurs the opportunity to make that transformation.

In such times, no one will complain about what you do. Even if you do something out of the ordinary, your employees will keep silent. So, difficult times are times of opportunities and times for dramatic reforms. If you do, I believe you will be able to open many more doors to the future.

Q&A Session

1

Urging People to Change Their Mentality

QUESTION:

In the current harsh economic environment characterized by phenomena such as deflation, there are people in the Japanese society, especially those over 50, who cling on to the postwar era of prosperity and cling on to the economic bubbles back when things went smoothly. They are unable to change their mentality. Please advise us on how leaders can instruct them and what kind of attitude leaders should have toward them.

The public will always come to realize
The situation later

RYUHO OKAWA:

In any age, it is the clever ones who notice things quickly while ordinary people don't even realize them.

Let's use the following example to illustrate the point. When they want to cross a railway line, clever people understand that a train is coming from a given direction before it actually appears, just by hearing it. Ordinary people realize that a train has arrived when they see it before their very eyes. There are also people who only become aware of that train when it has already gone.

Applying this type of logic to the different ways people see the world, the majority are those who notice the train when it has already left. Those who become aware of it when it is in front of them can still be considered above average, while people who know it is coming without even seeing the train are really clever. In this way, people's sense of awareness can be off by a number of years.

There is a reason why plenty of people have yet to gain a correct understanding of the present day. Japan's economy after 1990 is given nicknames such as "the recession decade" or "the lost decade."* Unfortunately, lots of people put up with the belief that it was the government's fault or the previous Ministry of Finance's fault. This is no good.

Although it is true that the government mishandled the economy, many people still think that such mistakes will not continue after a decade. They think, "Soon, there will

---

* at the time of the lecture.

be politicians like from the old economy heydays who will make a U-turn in policy and inspire the economy with goals like doubling incomes" or "Before we know it, we'll be in an inflation period again."

Since many managers are aged between 60 and 70 or so, they have experienced that era of high-level growth of Japanese economy. This is why they believed at first that this so-called "10-year recession" would be over in two or three years or that it's only a period of adjustment, so things would be back on track soon. They are surprised that it has continued for more than 10 years.

Even if they are told, "Certainly, this 10-year recession was a product of policy failure, but deflation itself is a structural phenomenon, so it's not going to go away," there will be people who respond, "Really?" or "I'll have to wait and see in order to believe that." In addition, there are people who only take notice when their company collapses. There are different kinds of people.

The statement, "The underlying deflationary trend is not going to change in the future" will surprise about 80 percent of people, who will only then realize how tough their situation really is. Still, most people will believe that a change in prime minister or help from foreign countries would solve the problem.

However, at its present state, the Japanese government does not have the strength to improve the economic climate. The U.S. starts a war whenever its economy goes down. This is because the U.S. will have to manufacture shells and missiles to be launched; the revenue of the defense contractors will increase dramatically. The U.S. government has enough strength to make the economy better.

However, Japanese politicians nowadays don't have the brains to think about generating consumption to improve the economy. They are so passive overall.

First, change your own attitude

In view of this, it is inevitable that common people's awareness of what's going on will be a few years behind.

Therefore, if you are a person managing a business or a person working in an enterprise and have already grasped what I have been saying, please change yourself first by modifying your frame of mind. If you do that, the company itself will change immediately, assuming you are the manager of a company with 10 or 20 people.

Although it will not be so easy if you are working in a large company, it is quite possible that at least your section or your department changes. People will start saying things such as, "That section seems to have changed a lot," "That department seems to have become quite different" and so on. Besides, if the change is not just a passing thing but is a continual sequence of visible changes, surely, the other sections and departments will learn from your changes, too. This will be a driving force that can save your company.

Of course, the best thing would be when these changes to your section or your department fall on the ears of the head of the company, but as I said earlier, most company heads are those who have experienced the periods of high growth; they cannot forget those times easily. It is useless because they will tell themselves, "Things will get better at some point and the old days will surely come back."

People who have entered the company in these tough economic times will see that this is not true, by the time they become management executives. However, this is a long way off into the future. It would be good if their company still exists then, but it is quite possible that the company no longer exists by that time.

So, you can only do what you can do now. The head of the company, department managers and section chiefs that have learned what I have said should put these principles into practice first. Alternatively, you could put this into practice even if you are a senior staff or an average company employee. If you change your working methods and improve your performance, the people around you will take notice. You should apply this everywhere.

The real proof of these principles will be shown by the progress of the companies applying the teachings of Happy Science, the companies that are engaged in this faith.

In Section 4 of this chapter, I talked about love, wisdom and self-reflection in the Fourfold Path. As for the aspect of progress, these teachings will spread further if you can prove through practice that those who have learned Happy Science are doing well, which in turn brings a lot of good. I want members and companies belonging to our group to progress and advance especially during these tough times.

Work at a company is not done alone. There are associations with clients and other people, so eventually they will be influenced. Thus, it is good to start and carry out whatever that can be done on your part.

2

Motivating Subordinates

QUESTION:

I would like to ask about the motivation of subordinates. In the past, people have offered various incentives and remunerations to subordinates in order to provide them motivations. However, nowadays it has become impossible to do so. It would be much appreciated if you would give us some hints to provide subordinates with positive motivation.

The motivation of supervisors will Spread to the subordinates

OKAWA:

In your question, you used the expression, "motivation of subordinates." I am sorry for being impolite, but usually, those who use that term are not so bright. Generally speaking, if their bosses are not that great, the subordinates will not be so motivated. Since it is true that people in higher positions are stronger than those in lower positions, if the supervisors are motivated, their motivation will spread to the subordinates no matter what.

191

Therefore, you cannot only blame the people in the lower levels. The subordinates are where they are because of their low level of awareness, because they possess little knowledge and have little experience. In fact, it is fundamental that the people at the top level motivate themselves as much as possible, so that eventually those at the lowest levels will change.

I am sorry for being strict, but in regard to the company heads, it is more effective to scold them. In most cases, praising them will make them worse off. By being told that they are no good, they will shape up and pull their act together.

Where do enthusiasm and a sense of mission come from?

If one examines various Japanese enterprises with atypical growth that developed after WWII, they all had CEOs with an atypical enthusiasm. This enthusiasm was not normal enthusiasm; it was different from the enthusiasm of the normal salaried office worker. All atypical growth came from CEOs with extraordinary enthusiasm.

It seems this enthusiasm at the top level comes from a sense of mission. This sense of mission comes from the fact that they are always thinking about the answers to the question, "Why does our company exist?"

If the CEO were to be asked, "Why is my company here?" "For what purpose does it exist?" "Why must it continue to exist?" and he answers, "So that the employees can make a living" or "So that I can continue to be the CEO," then he is an ordinary person. Such kind of answer is how a normal company would respond. "I hope that our company lasts, so that my workers can put food on their table and raise their family. I hope that our company lasts, so that I can continue to be the CEO" is an ordinary answer.

This is not enough. Even a small company with 30, 50 or 100 employees is sure to expand if they believe they will light up the world or the society.

There are many other contributing factors, but a company without this enthusiasm will not grow. People with such exceptional enthusiasm have centripetal force working on them. These people are magnetic, distorting the reality around them. It is as if people close by become magnets, too, so that the employees are magnetized and the business associates and other companies in the same business are drawn in. Thus, the company gets bigger.

However, if the top is easily satisfied with small success and feels, "This is enough," failure will follow.

A company that gets big will make yearly plans. If these are achieved, the CEO, executives, department heads, section chiefs and everyone working in the company are generally satisfied. "Well done! That's great. We will be paid our salaries and get bonuses as scheduled. This is good. I hope the same will happen next year and the year after next." Then they start getting passive, thinking, "I hope the company doesn't go bankrupt," "I hope it keeps up until I get married" or "I hope it doesn't go under until my kids have grown up."

But with such thoughts, they are more likely to be defeated. This is why you need passion. Passion comes from a sense of mission. A sense of mission comes from continuing to seek answers to questions such as, "Why does our company exist?" "Why should it continue to exist?" and "Why should this society, the country, and the world need our company?" Conviction, a sense of mission and passion are born within such managers.

To put it bluntly, most companies would not be missed even if they disappear, because there are many competitors. Companies will give excuses such as, "That isn't true. We're a long-running company," "We've been in business for 100 years" or "We're a famous company." But the question is, "Are you truly needed?"

Let's take Toyota as an example. At one point, Toyota's annual profit reached one trillion yen, but even that type of company would not be missed. Even if Toyota disappeared, consumers would not miss them if other companies that are currently performing poorly stepped up to fill the gap.

Toyota senses this danger; that's why it places emphasis on making *kaizen* [improvements] and makes efforts to achieve them.

If some companies and shops disappeared from the earth, that would cause problems for the people who worked there at that moment in time. However, there aren't many companies or shops that would be missed by people if they disappeared. Because there are competitors and other companies that would come to rise, people would soon switch to something else. As for TVs and cars, they can be bought from other companies. Clothes can be bought elsewhere. If farm produce cannot be obtained from your country, it can be bought from overseas.

It is for this reason that you must answer the questions, "Why must people keep buying our products?" and "Why should our company continue to exist?" Passion is aroused under a CEO who continues to think about the answers to these questions. Please think about this.

Answer the question, "Why is our company necessary?"

I believe it is a universal truth that subordinates lack motivation. More than 90 percent of people only want to work as much as they are paid. People who are motivated to work more than they earn are destined to have successful careers. People who rise up the ranks steadily are the kind of people who do more than what they are paid to do.

Nonetheless, most people do not rise up the ranks. People who do not have successful careers believe that working more than they earn puts them at a disadvantage. Those who believe they will not accomplish their mission unless they work more than they earn are those who leave their peers in the dust and succeed in their careers. Such people are always in the minority.

This is how things work within a company, but the company as a whole cannot improve unless it seeks to set itself apart from its competitors in some way. So, please ask yourself, "Is our company really necessary?"

I believe this is the same for religion. In the various utterances of people related to other religions in featured magazine articles, they say something like, "The economy is in hard times, so religions everywhere are in decline." These people are blaming deflation and the economic downturn.

Nevertheless, if you look back over the last 100 years, structurally, religions do well during periods of recession. The reason for this is that, in times of recession, more people turn to the gods or to Buddha since no amount of human effort can seem to turn the situation around. Times of recession are, in reality, times when religions do well.

However, many religions profess, "We can't get more believers because of the recession" or "We can't get income because of the recession." Religions are now very much the same as companies.

People will stop making effort when they blame the recession and deflation. However, it is not true that a lack of growth is due to recession; alternatively, it is not true that everything turns out badly because of deflation. Something neither expands nor grows because it is not needed. This is what it boils down to; the same goes for everything else.

Since any lack of growth for Happy Science would be because it is no longer necessary, we must continuously give thought to what the best course of action is in order to keep making Happy Science a necessary group and in order to make it even more necessary. Although I think about this too, every section chief ought to as well. Then, it will gradually trickle down to the lower levels.

I am sorry to tell you this, but most companies may not be missed even if they go bankrupt because they are not unique enough. Therefore, it is very difficult to claim that your company is absolutely necessary.

That is why you need to create something that will make your company absolutely indispensable and develop a philosophy that will nurture this kind of thinking. This will inspire all the employees and will make your company grow. There is a big difference between a company with a philosophy and a company without one. For employees to commit themselves to such a philosophy, CEOs and the managers need to keep asking the very basic question, "Why is our company necessary?" Keep asking this question, over and over again.

For instance, our international division would have to ask, "Why do we need to spread our teachings overseas?" If the staff in the division can answer this question, they will be able to increase the number of members overseas to as much as five to ten times as it is now. However, if they cannot answer this question, they will not be able to gain more than the number proposed in the annual plan. That's all there is to it.

The same applies to companies. The question must be answered. The thought given to the question will have an impact on the results.

It is simple. You do not need any money. You just need to answer the question. Why is your company needed? Why is your company necessary? Why does it need to survive? What are the reasons that the company does not collapse in a period of deflation or recession? Why do people want your company to stay in business? Why must your company's products and

A CEO Must Develop a Philosophy

| Why is your company necessary? | → | Sense of mission and passion | → | Supervisor's motivation spreads to the subordinates |

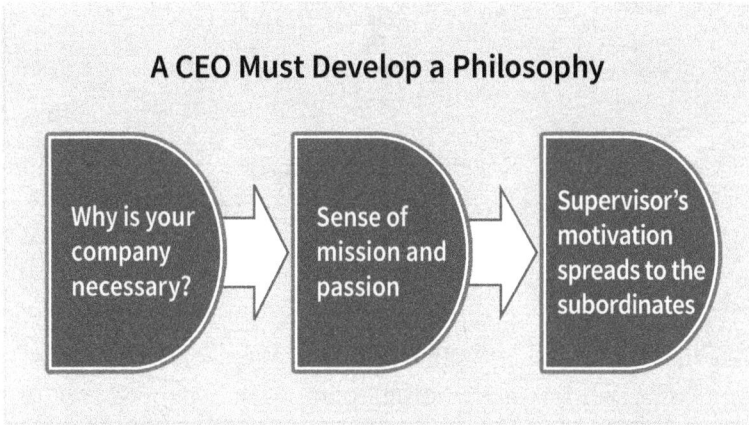

merchandise sell? Please answer these fundamental questions. The necessary course of action will become clear as you think about the answers.

I cannot give you specific advice because every company sells different product, so please think about your own situation. If you can answer these questions, your company will continue to grow next year, the year after that and 10 years from now.

3

Precautions on Conducting Businesses in China

QUESTION:

At present, there are many companies conducting businesses in China, while on the other hand, some people forecast the economic collapse of China. Please tell us what you expect to see in the two cases, while giving us precautions on conducting businesses in China.

Companies that fail in their country will not Succeed in foreign countries, either

OKAWA:

For a long time now, many companies have failed after moving operations over to places with cheap labor. Of course, starting a business in a foreign country involves country risk and political risk, which are difficult to deal with as an individual company. This is why it is true that things can get hopeless whenever a company becomes overwhelmed by the wave of major political change.

Now is the era in which companies should challenge and go abroad though being fully aware of such risks. Nevertheless, in principle, companies that think, "Since we're not having success on our own turf, let's succeed in a foreign country" are doomed to fail. There is no doubt about this. "Let's start elsewhere, let's find a means of escape. There must be somewhere we can be successful"—companies that think like this who flee from the struggle in their own country and try to battle overseas will fail.

There is no reason to expect companies that have failed in their own country to go abroad and enjoy success. There is no way for Japanese companies that fail in Japan, where Japanese is spoken, where they understand the culture and the customs, the manners, the geography, the suppliers, the sellers and what their competitors are doing, to go abroad and expect to succeed when they know none of these things. This is quite obvious.

The sole chance for success for such companies would be if they conduct their businesses in an area where no one else has ventured. However, they would go under the moment another company comes over to set up shop in the same business. It's as simple as that.

Those who are doing well in their home country despite the economic recession are the only companies that will do well extending their operations in a foreign country. If they go abroad when they are in danger of going bankrupt at home, they will fail. If they are in good shape at home while their competitors are all having a tough time and then go abroad, they will be successful.

In management terms, this is referred to as "dam management." Dam management involves water being held back by the dam and being allowed to flow through in times of necessity and being stopped when not needed. Companies that have major success at home, have acquired the know-how, accumulated capital, saved up various things, have money to spare and go overseas—such companies can afford to bear losses. They take into account how much they can afford to lose and still be well-off.

There is a difference between such companies and others, who are betting all their chances overseas. Even Toyota, a major corporation, moved some operations over to China and built a factory in Tianjin, then reported production figures of 30,000 cars for the first year; very steady. Even if Toyota were unable to sell any of those 30,000 units, it would be no big deal. It's steady.

However, dreamers always want to go big. Dreamers think immediately in terms of "millions of units"; such people risk the entire life of the company on wins and losses. The companies that actually do turn big profits like Toyota think, "Start small and steady. Only go big once you're well known." Places like these do well, but those that try to find a way out of their troubles by banking on opportunities presented by cheaper labor alone will collapse. This is the harsh reality.

The bottom line is to make profit In your main business

In this era, companies that adopt a mindset such as, "Since our main business is struggling, let's start up something new as a side business and thereby revive ourselves, get back into surplus and cover the balance that is in the red," are most likely to go bankrupt. As you would expect, your main business must be producing profits. This is the bottom line.

If your main business is not able to make profits and a side business is set up, it will only rob energy, wisdom and money away from the main business. Also, since a system incorporating new know-how is required, that is difficult, too. There is insufficient ability, so profits do not materialize. This will surely have an impact on the main business. Main businesses that are struggling now will end up struggling even more. If the main business goes under, it is virtually impossible to revive it. The only course of action is to transfer business to another field. This is how you must think.

If you, a manager, aim to achieve success with a new business since your main business is struggling, your company will most likely disappear within five years. On the other hand, you will usually succeed in starting up new ventures if you think, "Our main business is going well. We'll allocate some of our resources to a new project, but if by any chance it goes under, we shall remain unaffected."

Yet, as a basic concept or mindset, any new venture taken on should not be too irrelevant to the main business. It would be difficult to undertake the new venture unless it is in the same line of business as the main one. Therefore, in principle, I am opposed to reckless diversification as it leads to failure. Oftentimes, people who try things they are not accustomed to will fail.

In the past, a certain steel company established an eel-breeding farm on the site of a factory, but as you would expect, it didn't go well. There is too much of a gap between making steel and breeding eels. Even if you were to assume, "The land is vacant and there's a blast furnace, so we can produce hot water. We should be able to breed eels," since the employees there were not employed to breed eels, you would have to call upon the services of someone from the fishing industry. The basic content of the job is completely different.

In this way, putting into practice the idea of a complete novice does not make something possible. You could achieve something if it was similar to your main business. You could enter into a business sector that entails somewhat similar mindset. However, it's very hard to enter into a business sector that is completely different from your present one.

For example, it would obviously be difficult for a place like Happy Science to make a massive effort to produce things, since we preach, "It is the heart rather than material things that is important." We could make things that are related to the heart, but if manufacturing becomes the main subject, it will get tough because the concept is different. That's how it is.

Since deflation is basically going to continue from this point onward, a lot of people would immediately think about finding a way out somewhere new. However, that idea generally stems from the wish to cease taking managerial responsibility for the main business and put the blame on the environment, thinking that they will gain a new lease of life in a new area. It is safe to assume that there is a high chance that such thought will lead to failure.

The risk of conducting businesses in China
And what's to come

Conducting businesses over in China involves country risk. I truly believe so. It may be possible to raise profit by entering such a market, but should the political system change, you could forfeit the entire business. You could even get your factory confiscated by the state and be turned into a state-run business.

Therefore, it would be absolutely fine to start a business there if you do not mind losing everything and think, "Even so, it's still profitable." However, it's better for a company that thinks, "If we lose, we will go under" to not enter that market.

There are fundamental problems with regard to the evolution of the market in China. Since China is governed by a totalitarian one-party rule, even if its market economy develops to some extent, it is bound to collapse sooner or later. It will inevitably face the dilemma of making a choice between a market economy and totalitarianism.

Market economy is not compatible with totalitarian one-party rule. What is compatible with totalitarianism is a rationing system. In totalitarianism, the most compatible method is for the state to manipulate prices. In short, a regulated economy run by a military regime is the best method in a totalitarian system. Therefore, implementing a market economy is a threat to totalitarianism.

In China, there used to be a policy that people who establish a company should not become a member of the Communist Party of China. Recently, however, since such people are making good profits, the Communist Party has been planning to bring such people under control. For example, the CEOs of profit-making companies that manufacture computers are made to become CPC members or are being promoted to the top echelons of CPC.

Since the above process is tantamount to being brought under a regulated economy, it signifies a decline of the business. If a company is brought under the control of CPC because it is making profit, the company is sure to collapse. It's a scary situation.

If that did turn out well, then Hong Kong, which was absorbed into China, should be prospering. Nevertheless, Hong Kong is becoming weaker. If Taiwan also becomes absorbed into China, it will gradually lose its economic prosperity, too. This is due to the difference in mindset.

Market economy is based on the principle of competition between companies with different values, where the strong survive and the weak are eliminated. But such comparative thinking does not exist in the doctrine of the one-party rule system, so there is no way that a market economy can possibly exist.

Therefore, basically, it is very difficult to align totalitarianism with market economy. This is why the struggle continues in finding out which will win, politics or economics. Since there are 700 million people living in the agricultural communities of China, the political system cannot yet be overturned. However, if the free market expands, anything is possible. This kind of political risk will inevitably accompany businesses in China.

China's way of doing things is illogical, so it will not work out in the end. When the number of people making profit from the market economy surpasses 50 percent of the population, the political system may fall. There is no future for China unless its political system changes.

In China, at present, there are 600 million people living in cities and the urban communities while 700 million people are living in the agricultural communities. And since the level of economy of the agricultural communities in China is nearly the same as that of pre-WWII Japan, the CPC, with its main power over the agricultural communities, is not in danger of collapsing at the moment.

Nevertheless, the situation will flip as soon as the entire country shifts to market economy. The current system will be in jeopardy as soon as the market economy takes more than half the share. The present one-party rule system will definitely come to an end. Basically, one-party rule system only works to kill the economy. A regulated economy is the only system compatible with it. This is why the system will collapse.

China will eventually lose one or the other: politics or economy. History will prove which side prevails. The result will come in 10 or 20 years. However, I believe the basic trend will be that politics will lose.

Chapter Three

Introduction to
Top Executive Management

~ The ideals as top management ~

Lecture given on October 16, 2002

1

A CEO Must Be
His Own Private Power Generator

The CEO must be the energy source

In this chapter, "Introduction to Top Executive Management," I would like to talk about helpful topics for CEOs, those who work in positions that give management support or who aspire for such positions.

"CEO-logy" must cover extensive ground, but if we look mainly from the side of religion, the main theme probably comes down to matters of character and mental attitude. Thus, without going too deeply into technical matters, I would like to talk as far as I can from a religious standpoint.

The first thing I would like to say is that a CEO must be his own private power generator. Today, we rely on electric power companies to supply power to every household. As such, we know that the light turns on when we flick the switch, thanks to the power we receive from another source.

But this is not the way as a CEO. A CEO must generate his own power. Perhaps the scale will not approach that of major electric power companies, but you must be the source of your own "electric power."

"I receive electricity which enables me to turn on the light when I flick the switch"—this is the stance of an employee. "I get motivated when the boss fires me up." "I get motivated when I'm given directions." "I get motivated when I'm given a goal." All these ways of speaking of motivations are from the standpoint of an employee.

Who gives targets to a CEO? Who tells a CEO, "Go for it"? Usually, there is no one to say these sorts of things. Of course, in the case of large companies with many shareholders, it is only natural for a general shareholders' meeting to

**A CEO Must Be
His Own Private Power Generator**

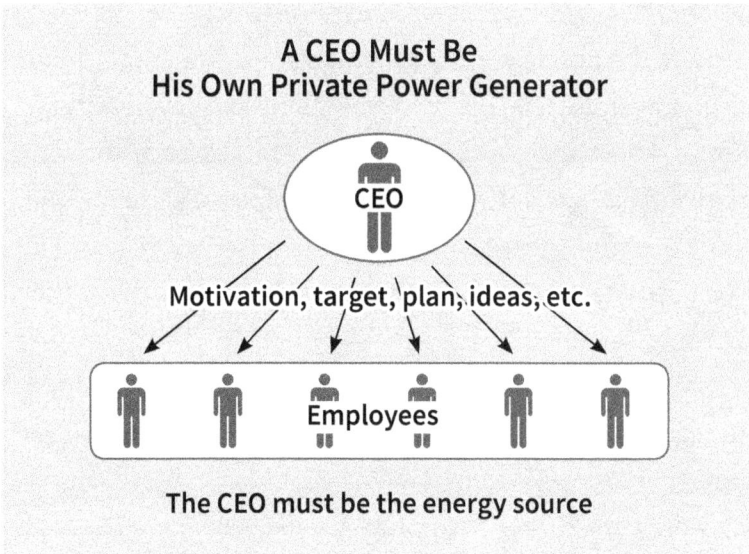

Motivation, target, plan, ideas, etc.

Employees

The CEO must be the energy source

demand the CEOs to be replaced if such companies run up a large deficit and this deficit continues over some period. This is because the CEOs will be asked to take responsibility.

Typically, answering questions such as, "What type of work shall we do?" are within the duties of the head. Objectives, questions about new ideas, how far and to what extent to go with certain ventures and so on, are issued from above. In short, the CEO must act as the supply source. Please understand that, regardless of your company being large or small, the manager or CEO must, by all means, serve as the private power generator. This is the first point I would like you to bear in mind.

Even if there are just ten employees, a CEO is a CEO. Of course, there may be situations in which the employees criticize the boss, but the fact remains that the supply source of energy must be the CEO himself. It is necessary for you to know that, as a CEO, your employees will not be motivated unless you give it your all, spinning the turbines and generating power. Why should those below, receiving lower salaries, bother to work hard if the person above them isn't motivated to do so?

Whether there are 10, 100, 1,000 or 10,000 employees in a company, the one standing over them must bear the following sort of thing in mind: "I shouldn't expect to receive my power from another; rather, I must generate and supply the power and energy on my own." You must operate the turbines by yourself rather than receiving orders from others. You cannot be a leader unless you are always willing to run the turbines in order to keep generating power.

People who lack the will to generate power themselves are those who, in short, only work hard when they have to such as in times of deficit or debt. Such people are not competent workers. Therefore, people who have lost the will to generate power by themselves ought to consider whether they should resign.

Department heads and section chiefs must be Private power generators, too

I have said that the matter lies solely in the hands of the CEO. However, in larger corporations, there is another side to this story. Of course, it is necessary for a CEO to think that he must generate power by himself, but in a large company, there are many positions, including department heads and section chiefs.

Accordingly, a department head must think of himself as the power generator for his particular department. He must think, "If the power does not come from myself as the department head, then this department will not be useful."

The same goes for section chiefs. If the section is composed of 10 or 20 people and the section chief is a lazy fellow, his subordinates will not develop any motivation.

So, it is necessary for those in the upper-level management to perceive of themselves as being private power generators. You should not only work hard when you receive the electric current. The CEO supplies the electric power, of course, but the department heads cannot simply wait for the power to be passed down to them.

They shouldn't say, "I haven't received directions from the CEO, so I won't do any work." It is wrong for section chiefs to do nothing until they hear from the department heads. If that is the case, the company will flounder. You must keep in mind that you need to be private power generators.

2

The CEO Bears Responsibility
For the Entire Company

The responsibilities of a CEO can be harsh,
But can also give a sense of purpose to your life

In this way, responsibilities will be shared with many people according to the scale of the organization. In small to medium-sized companies, however, responsibility rests with the CEO alone. In this regard, matters that may seem harsh are, in another sense, things that give a sense of purpose to your life. It is a splendid thing to operate a business at your own discretion. It is great to do things with your own ingenuity without anyone to give you directions.

No matter how small a company, the CEO deserves respect. Simply put, he can do things that others cannot. You can't simply appear from another company and become a CEO just like that. The CEO of a company has built up on all its achievements and knows all the work that has been done.

Although Happy Science is not a company, I have faced similar issues in running the Happy Science group. I had no teacher to guide me. Usually, a religious figure would begin to study under a teacher from a young age and eventually succeed the teacher upon his death. However, I had no teacher. This might be considered a tough thing, but I rarely thought of it in that way. Rather, I felt it was natural not to have a teacher.

For that reason, when I made a mistake or was not successful in something, I changed my way of thinking. By experiencing various incidents and witnessing diverse phenomena, I reflected and changed my way of doing things. I suppose you could say that there were times when my handling of a situation was not always preemptive. I could take preemptive action on things that I knew, but in regards to things that I had no knowledge of, I had to play catch-up. In my case, however, with regard to what I sent out, I could judge myself based on the results and change my ways as well as my thoughts. I repeated this over and over again.

The same exact thing can be expected of managers. You must take responsibility for the results of your own thoughts, ideas and actions. You must accept the challenge that comes with this responsibility.

You can make demands on your subordinates
If you think to yourself that
You are responsible for everything

A CEO is able to make demands on his subordinates precisely by thinking that he is responsible for everything. If the head takes no responsibility and simply says to his subordinates, "Get yourselves working," his employees will only work hard under his supervision. They will not put in much effort without it. This is only natural.

When the head takes responsibility, this means that he will be faced with responsibility for things that he did not do himself. This is tough. Yet, it is by thinking that you are responsible for things you did not even see, that you are allowed to make demands on subordinates.

A CEO must assemble his executives, gather department heads and clarify what it is that he wants them to do. If he does not do this, he'll be nothing but a scapegoat. If he has an idea of how he would do the job, he must make it known.

You cannot blame your subordinates for how things are not turning out the way you want them to if you do not make precise demands. However, it is ridiculous to simply admit and take responsibility for their failure, if it were due to you not making demands. You may feel, "If it were me, I'd do it like this," but in an actual work situation, the job will be carried out by other people. Therefore, you must make demands precisely. In this way, you are able to give orders because you take responsibility.

The same goes for a department head. It is only because he intends to take responsibility for his department that he is able to dispense orders to his subordinates, section chiefs or senior staff, "This is how I want you to do the work."

The subordinates who hear the demands of their superiors think, "Because the boss is taking responsibility, he delivers such tough instructions and demands, and sets up such high goals," and "Because the boss considers it his own responsibility, he makes these demands." Then, the subordinates feel they must live up to the demands.

However, if the subordinates feel the boss is shirking responsibility while telling them to get working, they will not work hard. They would think, "I can't do the job unless the boss makes me a department head." This is why those in higher positions—CEOs, managers, administrators, supervisors and so on—must first decide to take on responsibility for themselves before making use of their subordinates.

In order to instill drive in his subordinates, the boss must act as his own power generator. This means initiating your own proposals, using your own voice to express your enthusiasm and setting your own objectives. It is by committing yourself to take on responsibility that this enthusiasm shows in your demands, which then trickles down and results in a positive response from your subordinates.

If the boss completely lacks the will to take responsibility and instead simply gives orders and runs away thinking, "Don't rock the boat," his subordinates will also lack earnestness. If a department head who was scolded by the CEO hates being the only one to carry the burden and lets off steam by scolding his subordinates, they will act in exactly the same way toward those beneath them. In the end, everyone will only be thinking about themselves and try to avoid taking responsibility. Hence, this is a sensitive matter.

The head must take responsibility
Even for things he was not aware of

Be it a large company, the boss will quickly hold a press conference and resign with a bow when some sort of scandal occurs. Everyone knows that the person on top probably did not witness the event himself. We understand that in a company of 5,000, 10,000 or 100,000 employees, it is not possible for a CEO to know of every mistake that happens in a factory or to see in detail the cheating that may take place at some location.

As a CEO, you may want to go into the press conference and say, "This issue arose since the factory manager took up his post in factory X. Therefore, it is not my problem." If you were to say this, however, the mass media and the people watching the news would never forgive you.

People would say, "What are you talking about? Your company's name is all over. It is your company's products that are being produced. We know that you don't make the goods yourself, but you're working under the name of the company. You're working with the company's trademark. Thus, it is a matter of course that you take responsibility as the boss. In exchange for taking responsibility for things you are not aware of, you, as the CEO, get paid high salary and are honored with high social status."

You may want to assign responsibility to those on the spot and run away, but if you say this, you will not be forgiven. If you say such a thing, the company president won't be the only one to be blamed, but rather the entire company. The boss bows his head in apology in order to avoid assigning responsibility to the entire organization. By resigning gracefully, and in most cases by passing the baton to someone else, the boss aims to rejuvenate the company. This is how the affair is often settled.

People at the lower levels will get their acts together If the head's position is at stake

Those who are at the scene of the incident know that the head isn't fully aware of what occurs at the scene, so they might think, "The head will have to quit if we cause an accident or scandal because we cut corners. That would be horrible." Thinking in this way will cause them to become more mindful of their work.

Suppose there is a group of factory workers. One of them had a little too much to drink the night before. As a result, he daydreams the next morning and while working on an automobile assembly line, forgets to install a bolt or tighten it and the nut remains loose. Ultimately, that car leads to an accident that kills a person.

If the accident is a major one, it is only natural that the responsibility would fall on the head. The cause of the accident may in fact lie in the slack behavior of the person below which led to his poor condition caused by drinking too much the night before. The accident may have caused by neglecting a single bolt, but it is only natural that the top takes responsibility for any accident that occurs from the company's negligence.

Of course, if it is a small company made up of about five, ten or twenty people, the CEO can see everything and can be involved in all activities. Even so, if the CEO leaves on a sales trip, for example, employees may not do any work. It is uncertain whether he can see all that is going on. However, if the person on top avoids taking responsibility even a little, those below will also begin to do the same.

When the head always vows to take responsibility, those below will see this. If they think that the boss will take full responsibility no matter what happens, they will not sit around and do nothing even if they are not supervised. Thinking that cutting corners on their part will likely result in the CEO's resignation, they will refrain from doing so, even if the CEO does not make the rounds. This good tension, which affects and shakes up both sides, is very important.

Thus, to get right to the point, it is the boss' problem. The CEO must act as the power supply and think of himself as the one solely responsible. He puts forth ideas, plans and targets and takes full responsibility for the outcomes, even with matters that he does not personally oversee. He cannot get away with saying, "I didn't notice."

The responsibility of personnel appointments

In this regard, personnel matters are extremely important subjects of study for a company president. Since the company must run without having you to oversee every work, the task of the personnel section—of assigning people to different posts—becomes extremely crucial. The appointer is responsible for the work that the appointees' subordinates do, too. Responsibility falls not only on the people assigned to the positions, but also on the person who assigned them. In cases where there is even the slightest hint that people are not doing their job but still remain in their positions, responsibility falls squarely on the person who appointed them.

In short, these truly harsh aspects are the sole reason a CEO receives high compensation and public esteem. It may be impossible to substantially increase one's hours of physical labor, but the weight of responsibilities and the importance of the work change accordingly once one reaches the top. The question of how much responsibility the CEO must bear determines the scale of the company. It is related to the degree of scale to which the company expands.

Above, I explained how the CEO must be the private power generator and must adhere strongly to the principle of taking on full responsibility. A person who avoids taking responsibility by thinking of it as a problem of his subordinates is unable to make a company grow. In fact, that person will seek to pin responsibility on those outside the company. It will always be the fault of external factors or conditions. "Economy is bad." "The country's policies are to blame." "Foreign countries are to blame." "We were defeated because rival companies were doing such-and-such." The fault is always on external factors. Holding onto such perspective, however, won't make a company grow at all.

3

Failure Is the Best Teacher

You will always experience failure
When you try to break through your limit

Failure in itself is not such a bad thing. Failure is, in the long run, necessary for success. Only after experiencing failure, does the path to success open for people.

If one continually experiences success, it means that he has not given his all. The person may continue in his success until he reaches the limit of his abilities, but when he tries to break through that limit, he will definitely fail. Even so, you should not back down. Taking failure as your best teacher, you must take the hint and consider the following things: "What should I do?" "Where was the problem?" "What measures did I fail to take?" Failure is indeed the best teacher.

It is much less common for success to teach us to this degree. When you have success, you take it as self-affirmation. "I performed well, because I'm good at my job." "I'm a smart person." "It's because I have talent." "It's because we went with the prevailing conditions." These may be true, but they aren't of much help.

Failure, however, becomes a teacher. People ponder when they fail. They think deeply and repeatedly. This is important.

People who say they have never experienced anything but success have not pushed themselves to the limits of their abilities. For example, a person with the abilities of a department head working as a supervisor or a section chief may never fail. However, for both the person and the company, this is a waste of precious resource.

For instance, it is a real waste to have a person who could be a department head acting as a mere supervisor. If a person who could be an executive is stuck at the level of a section manager, it is either that those above do not have a discerning eye or that the person himself is not making good use of his talent.

People who say they've never failed should ask themselves the following questions. "Am I engaging my talents to the fullest? Am I thinking of breaking through the limits of my abilities?" "Am I just protecting myself? Am I relying on the idea, 'Don't rock the boat'; that is, the belief that I will be promoted so long as I don't fail?" Those in the upper reaches of an organization should also ask themselves the same questions.

A company with a leader who has never failed is also a company that cannot expand. Any venture enterprise will involve some measure of failure. In cases where a company is built within new business conditions or advances into a new industry, there will definitely be failure.

Anyone who is afraid of this cannot expect to advance into new areas. Those who are afraid of failure can only work in ways that they've always done. They will not expand nor flourish in new frontiers. Those who fear failure can have no further success.

Don't settle for the status quo; Make reasonable challenges That your company can handle

The boss must not fear failure, either. At the same time, the failure should not be too big for your company to overcome. If it is too big, then it will naturally be the end of the company. There is a limit to which a company can fail and still survive—for example, losing 10, 20 or 30 percent of its total strength.

Of course, failure should be kept within the endurable limit of an organization. Perhaps once in a lifetime, a company may find itself in a high-stakes, sink-or-swim situation. Even so, being in danger of annihilation, year after year, is too much of a risk; it is a gamble. That would be going too far.

Nevertheless, there are cases in which you may want to make reasonable challenges that your company can handle while recognizing the possibility of failure. We may say those who back down from such opportunities are coasting along in self-preservation. People who say they have never failed, may be boasting or getting recognition from others, but there seems to be a problem in putting their use.

Those who actively take on challenges will inevitably fail. There are people who understand this well and say, "Don't worry about making mistakes caused by active challenges." Those who take on challenges will surely fail, while those who do nothing will not.

However, in many cases of those who do nothing, the organizations employing such people will stagnate and soon die. Management will surely seek stability. It wobbles as it seeks equilibrium in times of turbulence. While stability is a good thing, do not settle for that, as settling leads to stagnation and decay.

While it is important to aim for stability, you should not aim for comfort. Once you feel that you have achieved stability, you must think of the next challenge. You must consider how to break through. Once stability is attained, you must next produce a small measure of instability to create strain on the organization and to provoke motivation.

If not, you will soon be unable to even maintain the status quo.

In today's difficult climate, only when you fight and fight can you keep the status quo. This is how it should be, so you must strive to have this attitude on a constant basis.

4

Management Philosophy
Brings Growth to a Company

A company cannot grow
Unless a management philosophy is implemented

In times of recession and rising bankruptcies, the managerial environment turns worse and people always turn timid. This leads to a situation in which everyone becomes timid and avoids taking new risks. You may have had courage when you established a company, but once it grows to a certain size, your self-preservation kicks in and you seek stability. Courage disappears as the company gradually heads toward maintaining the status quo.

We can see how this feeling might come about. As the number of employees working beyond your range of vision increases, you might feel, "No matter what I say or don't say, nothing will change." In addition, the number of people who refuse to take responsibility will increase.

Nevertheless, when you lose courage, you, as the CEO, must think carefully about the following matters. First, when a company is founded, the CEO's intention may be to do what he enjoys, feed his family, and make sure his employees have a full stomach.

Yet, as a company grows, this alone becomes insufficient. You must be prepared to answer why it is valid for your company to develop and prosper. This is because, as mentioned above, a CEO has no one to teach him such things. Having no teacher means you must figure it out by yourself. It is no use handing out a questionnaire to your workers.

Though it may be painful, a CEO must think by himself. "Why must my company grow from 10 employees to 50 employees?" "Our goal is to surpass an annual sales of 10 billion yen. Why do we need to do this?" This is where you need to think carefully upon the deeper meaning buried in such objectives.

This is called management philosophy, which is often lacking in small to medium-sized companies. Generally, in smaller companies, as the CEO thinks of himself as the sole manager, he is embarrassed for others to know the management philosophy since it is something like his own personal diary. Thus, he does not make his thoughts known to others.

However, a company cannot grow unless the management philosophy is implemented. Your company cannot grow as long as it is based solely on your own understanding, so you must rack your brain and develop a management philosophy. "For what purpose does my company exist?" "What, precisely, is involved in my company's growth? What are my intentions?" Such questions need to be thoroughly examined in the process of developing a management philosophy.

Despite this, in most cases, the CEO of a small company will say, "I have no need for such a thing. It's enough for me if I can stock up and make sales. As long as I can keep profits above debts, that's all I need." Many people think this way.

Nevertheless, when a company employs 20, 30 or 50 employees, these people will also need to have a purpose in life beyond work. In order for the company to make progress,

Develop a Management Philosophy

(Examples)

● Why must your company grow from 10 employees to 50 employees?

● Why do you need to surpass an annual sales of 10 billion yen?

● For what purpose does your company exist?

● What is involved in your company's growth? What are your intentions?

As you lay down the management philosophy, inspect to see if you have vanity, ostentation or conceit

234

it is necessary to have the courage to open up new paths; at the root of this courage is the management philosophy.

Righteousness will arise Once you lay down a management philosophy

Righteousness will arise once you lay down your management philosophy and convey it over and over again to your workers until they understand what the company works so hard for. When everyone in the company becomes aware of this righteousness, courage will arise.

Let's say that a company is based on a management philosophy that aims to solve environmental problems. If your management philosophy is to think about how to improve the environment, then you need to repeat this over and over again to your employees until they understand it thoroughly.

Thus, if your company philosophy is to develop the technology to solve environmental problems, you cannot remain satisfied with fulfilling small goals such as, "We are fine as long as our books show that we are in surplus." You will begin to think, "Right now, we use such-and-such technologies to protect the environment, but there are other technologies and we need to utilize those too."

Environmental problems include problems related to air, water and land, as well as habitats. Various types of environmental problems appear; therefore, as soon as you put forth an idea as an environmental solution, many other necessary and related tasks will appear. It is in this way that a company develops.

If you have laid down such a management philosophy, your workers will give their OKs when you say, "We need to push our company's sales from 5 billion to 10 billion yen. Then I would like to raise it from 10 billion to 30 billion yen." They will think, "I see. If we do not make our company grow, the Japanese environment will not improve."

Suppose there is a company whose job is to inspect and clean drainage water produced by a factory. The company's work does not end after simply cleaning the factory's drainage. If the company's goal is to clean up industrial waste water of the entire country, then the company must grow. If it is unable to expand, such technologies will not spread throughout the country.

This is one example. In this fashion, righteousness will arise once you lay down a management philosophy.

You will have the courage to make progress Once your righteousness arises

People get stronger once their righteousness arises. They get the courage to take a step forward and to expand.

If the CEO simply states his goal as pushing annual sales from five billion to 10 billion yen, those below will just think it is unrealistic. However, if he tells them, "There is nothing wrong with us growing in sales from five billion to 10 billion, from 10 billion to 30 billion, or perhaps up to 100 billion to one trillion yen in order to solve the environmental problems in Japan," they will think, "That's quite right. We will not be able to solve all of Japan's environmental problems unless we grow to that degree." They will aim to make the company grow and the workers in the sales department will be motivated as well.

They will think, "This is not simply a matter for our company. It is a right cause for the sake of Japan. Once we spread our company's environmental protection technologies throughout Japan, we must then send them out to the world." "China is heavily polluted and so is Southeast Asia. Africa may be lagging in terms of development, but things will get tough there from now on. Measures must be taken in these countries as well. There is more and more work to be done overseas. If we are having trouble spreading our technologies in Japan, we will not be able to expand overseas. We must work hard to grow quickly because environmental pollution is spreading around the world." With such thoughts in mind, technology specialists will give their best, as will workers in sales.

Furthermore, those who think it is sufficient to work only within the country will begin to say, "We must study English and spread our environmental protection technologies overseas." "China's factories are discharging pollution. The air there is extremely polluted and acid rain has become a real problem. We must export our company's technologies as soon as possible." In this way, you can expand your business.

Your management philosophy must not be Based on self-interest

As you can see, courage is indispensable for expanding your business. And at the foundation of courage is righteousness, which in itself is based on a management philosophy, as I have explained before. If you don't lay down a management philosophy, righteousness will not arise.

You have to think very carefully about your management philosophy by thinking, "For what purpose are we doing this?" If the purpose is rooted in the CEO's self-interest or egotism, the company will not be able to attract many followers or become courageous.

As you lay down this management philosophy, you must think carefully whether you are doing it for selfish reasons. "Am I doing all this out of self-interest? No, I'm not. I'm doing it for the interest of the public." If you do not maintain this way of thinking, your company will not grow.

Of course, even within the field of public interest, there can be "impurities." Among managers who think they are doing public work are those with hearts and minds filled with vanity, ostentation, conceit and so on. For this reason, with regard to public interest too, you must strive to look at things forthrightly and with clear eyes. Otherwise, you could make mistakes.

This is the state of 'non-ego' taught by Buddhism since ancient times, rather than selflessness. If your ego is strong and you strongly feel, "me, me, me," your vision will become clouded. You will begin to view everything based on whether it is profitable for you or not. When you see someone, you will not be able to see him as he truly is but only as how he might be of use to you. You see other companies and the society in the same way. But this is not a good way to be.

Buddhism teaches the state of non-ego. When you achieve this state, you reach *adarsa-jnana* [the great, perfect mirror-wisdom], a perfected state in which you feel as though you are a large mirror, and view the world as if you are reflecting it in that great mirror. You won't be wrong if you could see from this viewpoint.

Thus, it is necessary to examine whether or not there are problems in your aspiration to serve public interest, too. Even if you strongly assert that your company's growth is for the sake of society, this may contain elements of vanity and hypocrisy, or even deception or outright falsehood.

If you know that another company's technologies are better than yours, yet you continue to say that your company has the best technology, then you are engaging in deception. If you think that other companies have surpassed you or that they are producing superior products, you must reflect on yourself honestly and commit to producing better things. If it's your stated dream to have your company's technologies spread throughout the world and you see good products being produced elsewhere, you need to be forthright and acknowledge the situation.

If you fail to acknowledge this and instead continue to insist that your company's products are superior, that is where the ego shows. In this way, the self appears even within the sphere of public interest.

At such times, the organizational body must create "genes" that will pass on the message, "Let's make better and better products." Your management philosophy must not simply be a matter of singing your own praises or the praises of your company. In the management philosophy, there must be an element to make continuous progress. There must be the desire to lift up both yourself and your surroundings through continuous self-improvement and self-reflection.

You must not have a management philosophy aimed solely at growth. A management philosophy must contain something further and beyond selflessness or non-ego, in both personal and public matters. It must contain a desire to manifest what lies beyond these.

The thing that lies deep inside could be called either the ideal of Buddha or the ideal of God for people who have religious faith. For those who are not religious, this could be the ideal of humans, service to humanity or pursuit of happiness.

In order to keep impure thoughts out, CEOs must take a hard look at themselves and always be ready to reconsider things.

The best management is Consistent with the best religion

So far, I have stressed the importance of generating your own power, of the head taking responsibility and of the necessity of courage for company growth. I have also explained that righteousness is the source of courage and that a management philosophy is the basis of righteousness.

Your company won't grow much while you do things on your own, but if you feel you want to utilize many people to expand and develop your business, you will need a management philosophy that everyone would devote to. It is important to spend time and boil down your ideas before settling on a management philosophy.

In this management philosophy, you must surpass selflessness and non-ego, incorporating what we could call "the ideal of the universe." In the end, you cannot think solely in terms of your own company, but must rather aim to carry out a portion of the laws of the universe.

In this sense, the best management is consistent with the best religion. It becomes no different from religion.

In religion, it is necessary to have the object of devotion. Religious devotion is focused on an object of worship, sacred scriptures and so on—similar things are also found in a company. In a company, the management philosophy is equivalent to the fundamental teachings of a religion, while the CEO functions as the founder of that religion. If a CEO compiles his writings and speeches and turns these into reading material for his employees, this is equivalent to the sacred scriptures in a religion.

Nurture executives to be extensions of the CEO

Since spoken words fade out, when a business grows, the CEO will have to write things out and make them available to his workers. These must be things that will remain relevant, no matter how many times they are read or heard. Not only must you engage in the production of goods, but you must also create ways of thinking.

If the ways of thinking of the CEO are solidified and repeatedly expressed, then executives, department heads, section chiefs and so on can gain a deeper understanding of the CEO's thoughts and will be able to pass this understanding on to those below them. As such, your company will grow further if you can create a management philosophy and have your executives master it.

However, if you cannot accomplish this, meaning that the work begins and ends with the CEO, then your capacity for growth will be limited to what you can perceive. This range is also limited to the CEO's abilities. There are CEOs that can supervise up to 10 people, 50 people and 100 people. In rare cases, people can supervise as many as about 300 people, but there are, of course, limits to the abilities of a single human being.

Therefore, how much a CEO can make his company grow has to do with creating extensions of himself. In order to create extensions of the CEO, it is necessary to nurture executives who are able to make decisions founded on the same ideas as the CEO's.

For this purpose, you must put forth a foundation for decision-making, similar to the sacred scriptures of a religion. The person on top must always make his way of thinking clear to others. It is important to boil down your way of thinking, present it to others and have them understand it. If you cannot do this, your company will not grow.

In general, there are many talented people among CEOs. In an owner-operated company, the CEO is generally treated as an almighty figure, be it a small company with several employees, or a bigger company with 10, 50 or 100 employees. This is both a positive feature of owner-operated enterprises and also a limiting factor, as the range of the work that the company can do is limited to the abilities of the CEO himself.

Thus, the next thing you must do is to develop a system in which you do not have to have your hands in everything. This is why it is important to create a management philosophy as I have discussed above.

5

The Struggle Against Limits of Ability

In a rapidly developing business, Some long-time workers become useless

As a company develops, there is a possibility that those who were useful in the past become useless. This is unfortunate, but it cannot be helped. There are limits to people's abilities, so as the company passes over these limits in the course of its development, it becomes inevitable that some people will be left behind in terms of ability. Some companies will experience this at some point in time.

If the company's rate of progress is very high, the number of workers left behind will increase. Then it will become necessary to replace them with workers of different types. New circumstances will call for people with different capabilities, so you must keep a sharp eye out for people you need.

For example, let's say a company produces a number of hit products and grows into an unexpected size. Riding the wave, the company has produced good products and has grown by achieving great success in sales. However, if the company has not made preparations appropriate for its expansion, there will be workers left behind in various places.

Therefore, it is true that sometimes a company will end up with black-ink bankruptcy because its sales went up too well. To be able to sell products well is something that we should be thankful for, but in cases of unexpected success, a company can go bankrupt while in surplus due to insufficient preparations.

You must be calm and understand that in a company undergoing rapid progress, some long-time workers become the useless ones. If you are not aware of this, company management will come to a dead end.

This is when emotional matters appear. There will be cases such as an employee who had been the president's right-hand man only five years ago become incompetent.

This, however, signifies the company's growth. If you have a management philosophy or a just cause, for instance, to solve environmental problems all over the country and truly wish to realize that goal, you must bring in more competent leaders by promoting people who possess superior level of ability or newly hiring such people. If you do not do this, you will not be able to get to a higher level and your desire to solve your country's environmental problems would be a lie.

If your cause is just or if you truly possess a righteous management philosophy, you will be able to make selfless judgments in promoting or hiring capable people. However, without a management philosophy, your company will merely be a body of common interest in which the workers will think of profits as something shared among them. In such a case, there will be resistance from those who wish to protect their own interests and, ultimately, there will be no progress.

This is where you are asked whether you can overcome a hurdle. There would be no workers falling behind while a company remains small, such as growing from 20 to about 50 employees. But quite a few of them would fall behind if a company of 20 employees breaks through to that of 100 employees. This is also true of a company that reaches 300 or 500 workers.

The boss will also reach the limits of his ability

It is not merely a matter of an expanding workforce; you will also see hurdles in terms of sales. The first hurdle to cross is an annual sales of about 100 million yen. Some companies are unable to reach that amount, no matter what they do. This may well be a matter of their president's skills.

The next wall is an annual sales of one billion yen. Once that is surpassed, the 10 billion yen wall will appear. Very few businesses are able to top an annual sales of 10 billion yen. Very few businesses can surpass this amount. Like a salmon swimming upstream, the number of successful businesses steadily dwindles with each successive hurdle. There is a wall for the number of employees and one for the annual sales.

At these times, you must carefully consider whether you have what it takes to be the boss of a company with an annual sales of one billion yen, 10 billion yen or 100 billion yen. If you find that your capabilities cannot be pushed further, one thing you can do is to think about how to survive within the range of your capabilities.

Look objectively at your own work without your ego coming into play. Do you feel that you can grow further like Japanese automobile and electronics manufacturers who were able to expand in the postwar period? If you believe so, you must steadily change your thinking and shed your old skin for new. Unless you do this, you will not be able to succeed.

At such times, as mentioned above, some of your employees who you have relied upon will become useless. You, the president, will also hit the limit of your capabilities. In small to medium-sized companies, the limit of growth usually comes from the limit of the president's capabilities. Success is attributable to the president's capabilities, but so is the limit to the company's growth. I have said that

Always Fight Against Your Limits

Wall for annual sales, wall for number of employees, etc.

The wall limiting company progress can be broken if the head innovates and makes a breakthrough in his own abilities

<Examples of innovation by the head>

● Change way of thinking and behavior

● Cast off old characteristics and replace them with new ones

responsibility must fall with the president himself. Also, the company will see the limit to its growth in accordance with his capabilities.

Yet, there is a tendency among CEOs to deny this. They do not recognize these limits, do not want to know these things or talk about it. They do not want to hear negative words or criticisms.

Suppose you say, "My company has reached an annual sales of 300 million yen. How about that? That's really something, isn't it?" However, if you hear someone say, "What are you talking about? Lots of places have annual sales of 2 billion or 3 billion yen," you would get angry. In this way, it is a trait of a CEO to boast about the current success of his or her own company without considering other companies.

So, the president could become useless, too. In a large company, there are supervisors, department heads, section chiefs, and so on who become useless. The same thing happens to the president as well.

In order to prevent this, you must seek in advance the aforementioned state of adarsa-jnana, where, like a huge mirror, everything becomes reflected. You must look at the images of yourself, your company and what's going on around you, and seek the way you and your company should be.

If your company is in a state where it can seek a higher stage of development, you must shed the skin as a CEO of a company with an annual sales of 100 million yen and become a CEO of a company with an annual sales of one billion yen. It is necessary to consider the ways of thought and necessary behavior of a company with one billion yen in annual sales.

Furthermore, in order to raise your annual sales of one billion yen to 10 billion yen, you must possess views that are appropriate for a 10 billion-yen company. Therefore, you must cast off your old characteristics and replace them with new ones. Otherwise, you will no longer be able to stay as CEO. Please know this as a fact.

Here is where the issue of management philosophy comes up once more. You will be in a struggle against your instinct to protect yourself. You will ask yourself, "Am I doing the right things as the boss? Am I doing anything wrong?" When you, the head, innovate, shed your old skin and keep developing, the company expands; when you reach your limit, the company will stop expanding. At such times, based on your management philosophy, you may have to consider about retiring.

A great majority or about 97 percent of the companies do not grow very large, just as the size of a crab's nesting hole depends on the size of its shell. However, a small number of companies will grow to a considerable size.

You, the boss, must always battle against the limit of your abilities. Being the boss is fulfilling, but at the same time, it is very challenging.

Every CEO will come to the limit of his abilities, No matter how excellent he may be

Some excellent CEOs in Japan indeed had a limit to their capabilities, even though they were regarded as not having one.

For example, Soichiro Honda, founder of Honda Motor Company, appears to be the hero of his generation. Yet, he also had a limit to what he could do. While he had knowledge in mechanical production, he lacked knowledge in electronics. When the age of electronics arrived, he realized he could not continue and quickly retired. He knew that his time was up and no one can do well in the industry without specialized knowledge of electronics.

Konosuke Matsushita, the founder of Panasonic, did not become useless all throughout his life. In his later days, however, he said, "I don't understand any of the products my company makes." That's the way things go. Someone with the knowledge that dates back to when the two-way socket* was invented will in no way understand the advanced, cutting-edge products being produced at the time.

Then there is the founder of Sony, Masaru Ibuka, whose company grew out of his hobby with wireless radio and gradually became bigger. In his later years, however, he became involved in early childhood education and established a research center dedicated to the study of psychic powers. "These powers will be the main trend in the 21st century," Ibuka said. "We need to do these things in order to grow." So, he got involved in the study of psychic powers.

His workers at Sony said, "Our founder is getting old and a little senile. Well, we cannot do anything about it, since

---

*A household appliance invented in 1920 by Konosuke Matsushita. The device enabled the use of two appliances from a single electrical socket. It was a major hit in the early days of Matsushita Electric.

he is the founder. We can let him have his fun as long as he doesn't do serious harm to the company." In this way, Ibuka was allowed to do as he pleased.

I do not think Ibuka's ideas were very weird. He established the company and invented machines in the beginning, but as the years passed, he probably felt that machines can only do so much. Thus, thinking that it would be no good to make advancements in technology if it made people lose their heart, he turned his attention to eastern medicine and psychic powers. He studied things such as the *qi* in *qigong*.

Is qi made up? No, it is real. Eastern medicine, in particular, is truly useful. Most people who become too immersed in mechanical things and accustomed to Western technology deny the existence of things like qi and psychic powers. Hence, Ibuka thought that this will lead to a limit in human progress. The founder said these things, but his employees turned a deaf ear. This is how large his company had grown.

Therefore, while the spirit on which a company was founded can go on, as time passes and the company steadily grows, different abilities will be required. This is something you must understand.

Shifting toward developing the ability
To leave tasks to others and judge their performance

Only one company in a hundred might make it this far. Even so, when a company grows beyond its expectations, the CEO must start making efforts to stay as CEO by making innovations to his capabilities.

If, however, he feels he cannot keep up with the rapid progress no matter what he does, he must devise a way to delegate work to others. You must have the virtue that allows you to utilize other people.

Even if you are unaware of the detailed techniques, you must be able to make judgments on other people's capabilities based on their entire character as the one in command. You must be able to answer the question, "If we leave it to that person, will he succeed or not?"

Furthermore, you must entrust your subordinates with the task you used to do. So, you must concentrate your energy on judging how well they perform in their work. Although you may be upset and think, "I can do this, but you can't. So you're no good," you must gradually leave things to that person and shift toward developing the ability to set objectives and judge their performance. In this way, the content of your work will change.

Soichiro Honda made the rounds, even after his company became huge. When he saw something wasn't being done well, he would say, "Can't you even drill a hole for that bolt to fit into?" If a younger employee replied, "We can't do it if you don't show us how, sir," he would say, "OK, I'll show you how." He then would go under the car to drill the hole and tell them, "That's how you do it." He probably remembered how he used to do that in the past.

But in general, a growing company will eventually come to the stage in which that sort of ability alone will no longer be useful. You have to think about how the contents of your work will change according to the size of your company. At first, you have to do the work yourself because there is no one to do the work for you. Nonetheless, as things become settled, it gets important to delegate work to others.

Next, while delegating work to others, you must judge their performance and employ your energy into working out the best way for them to achieve better results. By delegating work, your task becomes to evaluate how well your workers perform. Your task would not be to think about how you would perform the task yourself, but rather how to get your workers to do even better.

Expand your capability,
So that you can make use of people with high skills

Moreover, you need to have a large capacity in order to make use of people with skills. In a growing company, people with skills will keep coming in, from the CEO down to the executives, department heads and section chiefs, creating an intense competition of skills.

Things will not go well if, at that time, for example, the department head is jealous of the section chief. Skilled people are coming in because the company has grown since the time the department head was a section chief. If superiors are jealous toward their subordinate, the company will not be able to progress to the next level.

As a company grows large, there will come a time when those above can no longer defeat those below in terms of technical skills and knowledge. Newer or younger people have more knowledge in the technical field, but all that those above need is to be superior in the overall sense.

Due to phenomenal progress in machines and so on, CEOs over 60 who are at big manufacturers are having a difficult time. Things have completely changed from the past; the knowledge they learned from textbooks has become nearly useless. Going back to learn things anew is a tall order.

The number of things you do not understand or cannot do only grows as your company grows or your position goes up.

If your company is small to medium-sized, you may feel you can do everything as the almighty leader due to the great skill gap between yourself and your employees. However, people who possess greater technical skills and knowledge or who have studied the new disciplines will gradually appear. You must make use of these people. This is a serious matter.

You must be able to endure not being able to do or understand something and still produce results. This is something you have to do and this is where management studies or the know-how steps in. You need to experience this in order to learn about such matters. Management experience and knowledge can only be gained when you are placed in that position. No matter how experienced you are as an engineer, you do not have the management know-how until you have been in a management position.

Ex-engineers can become exemplary managers, too

In general, most engineers are not well suited to become managers. Yet, if we look at postwar Japan, we see that excellent CEOs were frequently ex-engineers.

New technologies are constantly developing, so an engineer who tries to get by solely on his own skills will gradually become unable to work. However, he cannot simply study the new technologies together with recently graduated students.

At such times, you must innovate yourself to allow those who possess the most recent know-how and knowledge to work freely and to display their capabilities, so that more technological progress can be made. Thus, you must create a good environment for them, prepare the soil and look after them in various ways, so that they can produce results. Only those who employ their energy in this direction and transform themselves into managers can expand their companies and become exemplary managers of engineering background.

If such postwar Japan's CEOs had been obsessed with technology only, their company would not have grown. Those who survived recognized their own limits, i.e., they endured their lack of skill and lack of knowledge and directed toward figuring out what it is they can do.

For example, let's suppose you were to tell someone who makes huge machines to attach to state-of-the-art rockets, that you too, invented something in the past and show him something like a two-way socket. He would say, "This was a huge deal in those days, but times have changed" and laugh at you. The world of technology is one of steady progress.

The more recent things are definitely more advanced, so we cannot say that old things are better. In the case of religion, many old things are superior, but in the world of technology, newer is definitely better.

The same is true with medicine. If there were a parent and a child, both of whom are doctors, it would be common for them to quarrel because the information in textbooks in the child's generation are quite different from that in textbooks in the parent's generation. Since the contents have changed so much, the child will inevitably tell the parent that his knowledge is old-fashioned and will not get along well.

The same goes in the field of technology. Times change; things of the past usually become obsolete. This is something that you must accept. If the present rate of technological progress continues, nothing will last for a whole generation, or 30 years. Perhaps not even a single decade.

You must continue to study and absorb new know-how as technology progresses, but if you look at the present pace of progress, even doing such a thing will not be enough for you to keep up. At such times, younger people of greater abilities will appear, so you must direct your energy into letting these people work unhindered and create conditions for their success.

Know your limits and your destiny
And seek an ideal outcome

A CEO who fails at this sort of innovation must promptly make clear that he will retire. If it so happens that your company has a management philosophy as discussed above and if it serves public interest, then you must find some way to narrow the scope of your activities or retire the moment you think your limits are keeping your company from growing further. You need to consider this very carefully.

Although every manager is an excellent person, each has a point of limit in his ability. A store manager could be good at his job, but it gets harder and harder to keep an eye on everything when the store grows and opens two, three, five or 10 branches. You could have great business insight where you can personally oversee things, but they are bound to go wrong in situations you cannot keep your eye on. Mistakes will arise as long as you employ people and make judgments based on their reports.

Suppose you are a talented person who can instantly figure out the best course to take upon witnessing things firsthand. When a store grows in branches and other people are put in control of these stores and their many employees, you will need another sort of know-how. This is a difficult matter.

Know Your Limits and Your Destiny and Seek an Ideal Outcome

Do you think you can still grow?

> If so, you could fight and break through your limits

Do you think you are unable to keep up?

> If so, you could devise a way to delegate work to others
> 1. By acquiring virtue
> 2. By developing the ability to set objectives and judging worker performance

> If so, you could survive within your range of capabilities

> If so, you could retire

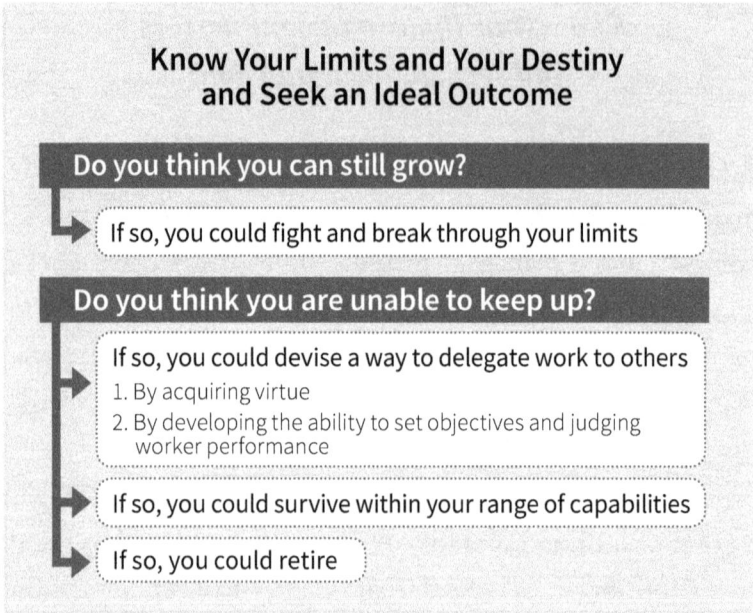

If you cannot succeed at this type of innovation, your company will not grow. Nowadays, making a company grow larger is not the only skill required. You can stick to defending your company or, if necessary, narrow its scope. This is one path that you can take. It is important to know your limits and your destiny and seek an ideal outcome.

I have spoken of various matters. I hope these will serve as a guide to top executives.

Q&A Session

1

Tips to Grasp Customer Needs

QUESTION:

Given that present conditions for business administration are tight, I think it becomes important in this situation to figure out how to grasp the needs of the customers. Please give us some general tips or tricks for understanding their needs.

Maintain the attitude to keep seeking

OKAWA:

This is something that everyone wants to know. To understand this is to have something of great value. If there were a seminar to teach you assured ways to grasp customer needs, such a seminar would likely charge a minimum of 100 million yen [one million dollars].

Grasping customer needs may be somewhat related to the luck that I spoke of earlier in this chapter. One who has good luck will quickly understand the needs of his customers. We might also refer to this as a manager receiving inspiration. People with a good sense or inspiration or people who are able to notice things a year or two before others are blessed with good fortune.

The basis of that luck is inspiration. There are people who see the same things but lack inspiration. It is important to be able to sense something. What do you feel when you ride a train? What do you feel when you ride a bus? What do you feel when you walk down the street? What do you feel when you watch a TV commercial? What do you feel when you watch a show on TV? What do you feel when you read a book? What do you feel when you read a book by Happy Science on theories of success and management?

Some managers could read a book and find something inspiring while others find nothing from the same book. This is not the fault of the author. In a book, some people detect a need while others do not. It is at this point that a person's luck as a CEO comes into play. At the root of luck lies inspiration; hence, it is important to find inspiration in whatever you encounter. This is also the power of each person's guardian spirit or guiding spirit, the latter being higher in spiritual grade. In this way, for the purposes of detecting needs, good luck is necessary—and at the base of luck is inspiration.

You may ask, "How can I get inspiration?" It is natural that inspiration comes from the fermentation of things that have been accumulating in a person's mind. Therefore, seen from this angle, it is important to maintain the attitude to keep seeking.

Those who are always seeking a need will be able to spot needs, but those who do not seek a need will not. Those who get inspiration are those who are constantly seeking, so the important thing is to keep seeking. Inspiration will come to those who continuously pursue a need and try to seize every opportunity, such as while watching TV, listening to the radio, walking down the street, taking a bath and so on.

In terms of secular ability, the things inside your own head can also provide you with inspiration. If you are always seeking the information you need, helpful information will pass into your eyes from the things you read or into your ears from the things you hear. Inspiration will come from such things. In short, it is important to have the attitude to keep seeking. This is the first point.

Receiving advice from the heavenly world

There is something else related to a person's attitude to keep seeking—prayer. Those who pray receive an answer, while those who do not pray receive no answer. This is the truth, although you may think it sounds unfair.

This is obvious to someone like me who has spiritual abilities. When you pray, an angel appears and tries to help you, but if you do not pray, an angel will not come to help you. Angels are busy too, so they leave it up to us to decide whether we need help. They do not interfere when they are not called upon through our prayers.

So, you can be certain that your prayers to the angels in Heaven are answered, but not answered if you do not pray. Even a spiritual being who does not usually come to your rescue will come when you call his or her name and pray. This really happens.

In essence, it is natural for inspiration to include things that come from the heavenly world. Among the best CEOs of the past several decades, there have been many who wanted to pass on their knowledge to the current generation and who, even after passing away, would like their know-how to be transmitted to others engaged in the industry. These spirits provide advice spiritually to those who are constantly polishing their ideas of management and who are seeking inspiration.

One characteristic of the Spirit World is that you can see what is to come more quickly than you do in this world. As I mentioned earlier, if you keep searching, you will discover things yourself. This is one thing, but another is that you receive advice from the Spirit World as you continue to seek.

Following is the method to receive advice from the Spirit World. First, you have to be seeking earnestly. Next, you must have an unclouded mind. You must seek sincerely and with an unselfish heart; put simply, seek with the idea that you must work for other people and for the society. If you do this with sincerity, there will be a response. But if there

Grasping Customer Needs

Constantly seek customer needs ➡ Inspiration

1. Keep searching and discover things by yourself

- Through fermentation of things that have been accumulating in your mind
- If you are always aware, you will receive helpful information

2. Receive advice from the Spirit World as you continue to seek

- Sincerely and earnestly seek assistance from the heavenly world (pray)

is selfishness, including thoughts such as, "I want to live in luxury" and "I want to look good," then no advice will come from the heavenly world. Conversely, in this situation, the advice you receive may come from demons.

This is why business management calls for spiritual discipline. While it is important to give as much worldly effort as you can on a constant basis, during seminars at a Happy Science temple, you can expect this advice to come down to you if you sincerely seek assistance from the heavenly world. You should create this kind of opportunity yourself.

Happy Science is a religion that is capable of receiving advice from any CEO who has returned to the heavenly world. Therefore, if it is necessary, you can certainly get advice from various spiritual beings.

A CEO in the Spirit World who is of the bodhisattva class is more than willing to help human beings. If a business appears to be heading for bankruptcy or a CEO wishes to develop the company, such kind of spirit will want to give advice. In order to receive this advice, you need to have suitable means of reception. At Happy Science, you can find many opportunities for management seminars and so on.

Here, I have discussed typical matters.

2

The Secrets to Innovation

QUESTION:

In the present context of violent transformations in social conditions, I believe innovation is necessary for businesses to deal with them and to keep developing. Please give us advice on what to keep in mind as we strive to make continuous innovation or on practical keys to innovation.

We live in an age ruled by speed

OKAWA:

Looking at present management conditions, we can see that speed is the ruling factor. Conditions are rapidly changing. It would be great if the same models of cell phones, TVs and computers could be sold for 10 or 20 years, but new products appear soon after and old ones quickly become obsolete. The lifecycle of products is very short, to the point where many devices become obsolete before they are sold and are discarded as heaps of garbage, causing environmental issues.

In the past, companies with lots of capital or many employees were strong, but this is not so today. Strong companies are the ones that can change quickly. Since large companies typically change slowly, a strong trend has emerged suggesting that being of large scale is a handicap. If a large company does not make every endeavor to increase its rate of change, it will inevitably fail. If you understand this rule, you can clearly see that expediting changes is important.

Looking at the ratio between the rate of change to the actual results, if, for example, a company is able to produce in a single year a new product that normally takes two years to develop, the ratio would be two-to-one. This offensive capacity would be squared to four-to-one in the actual marketplace. With a speed that is three times faster, the capacity becomes nine-to-one. This is how much difference there is.

Accordingly, it is crucial to shorten the time. However, since there is the dilemma that the larger you get, the slower you become, most companies are not able to grow large and be faster. For this reason, if you can resolve this inability, you can gain a victory over all others.

Small companies may have speed, but on the other hand, their administration is not very stable. There is a very high likelihood that their business only comprises a gamble.

First, you must plant firmly in your head the idea that we

have entered the age in which speed rules. "Those who are slow will lose. In order to keep up with changing times, you need to seek speed in everything you do. Otherwise, you will not succeed." A CEO must understand these sorts of things.

Be determined to protect things that should not change

As such, it is important to realize that we have entered an era of innovation. But that alone will lead to you losing your stability of mind or peace of mind. Therefore, while keeping in mind that you must constantly change, you must also hold onto the things that must not change. If you do not, you will not have stable prosperity.

At the same time, you must search for those things in your company that must not change. If you do not remain steadfast in holding onto those things that must not change, your mind will be shaken and things will go badly. If the change that takes place puts everything in complete and utter confusion, this is also a path to destruction.

For instance, let's say that a traditional *ryokan* [a Japanese inn] was rebuilt using reinforced concrete. Would the inn be successful? That alone would not be enough to bring success. At the same time, you should seek the things that should not be changed.

You must have the following as a fundamental policy or an idea. "Our company will not yield in regard to *this*. However as much the world may change, we must continue to hold onto *this*."

Be fast and detailed

Yet, you should observe how businesses change and how people's needs change. Then, you should practice time-based management and make the first move on the things you believe are OK to change. This is why it is necessary to be diligent and ardent in research and development.

A CEO must know that time is the most scarce management resource today. Not money, the number of people, nor factories or raw materials—time is the most valuable management resource. Those who give a thought to making things move faster are the ones who will succeed the most in today's world. You must look at things from this point of view.

Accordingly, you are right to judge that any company that works at a fast pace will grow. Of course, it is not good to be quick and dirty. Work that is done quickly is usually sloppy. It is both common for slow work to be detailed and quick work to be careless. Companies that are fast and

> ## What to Keep in Mind as We Make Innovation
>
> ● Make efforts to expedite changes
> ● Firmly hold onto things that must be sustained, such as a fundamental policy or an idea
> ● Study how businesses change and how people's needs change
> ● Be fast, accurate and detailed

detailed, in other words, companies that can integrate two completely opposite elements, will win.

Being slow and careless is surely a way to failure. This is a matter of natural selection.

Slow but detailed ones are on the borderline of survival. While those who do slow but accurate work may eventually be weeded out through natural selection, those who are slow and careless are destined to disappear entirely.

In the case of being fast and sloppy, you may be able to profit from going straight to the promising part of your current business, but this is not a recipe for stable progress. In that case, since it is impossible to enlarge on stable business connections, you will lose if other companies start producing more detailed work. If people say you work fast but are sloppy and make many mistakes, it will not be long before you disappear.

If you are able to resolve the contradiction by being fast, accurate and detailed, surely the virtue of your company will shine forth.

Additionally, you must also remember the necessity to resolve the contradiction between things that cannot change and things that must change, as I have stated earlier.

3

Criteria for Starting a Successful Business

QUESTION:

Nowadays, with various changes taking place in the business environment, there are many people considering quitting their jobs and starting their own company because it has become difficult for them to work their whole life for the same company. Thus, please give me your advice on the most important things to keep in mind when starting a business.

There has been a change in what kind of character And nature are sought in business people

OKAWA:

This is related to the previous question; compared to the period of rapid economic growth, what are believed to be of positive character and nature are totally opposite of what they used to be. Recently, several large companies in Japan have gone belly up. They were all prestigious companies people dreamed of working for.

The reason such companies went down is that the things being sought have changed. The sort of companies mentioned wanted their employees to work stably for a long period and perform well. But as I explained in my answer to the previous question, those companies did not ask their workers to speed up their work. People were hired at 22, did 40 years of service and became an executive at around 60. In this way, people achieved success via slow, gradual process of climbing up the ladder. Those who were in too much of a hurry to be successful dropped out of the system. All those who wanted to reach self-fulfillment in less than five years would drop out and start their own company.

Ordinarily, those who move slowly up the incline or those who think, "If I go at this speed, I'll be able to become an executive by the age of 60" will hang on in the company. However, those who go too slow will vanish and those who move too fast will also fall away. Companies had such generally expected promotion rate. This is why major companies do not only take on people with high levels of ability, but also see people as excellent ones based on their capacity to endure the gradual promotion.

If those with the ability to deal with rapid changes enter a company in such an age, in most cases they would be driven out as unwanted people. They would be told, "You're doing damage to the company, so please quit" or people

People Who Are Apt to Succeed in Starting Up a Company

● **People who have the ability to plan things**
➡ Those who can think laterally and put forth diverse ideas

● **People who live at a faster pace**
➡ Those who think and act much faster than others do

> You must have higher abilities than those valued as elite employees

around them wouldn't be able to stand them unless they were transferred somewhere or deprived of a role.

However, things have changed since the era in which people were called excellent and valued for taking decades to achieve self-realization. That being so, the type of nature that is sought has also changed. The sort of nature sought now is the type that was not valued until recently. Now, the tendency is to value such people highly.

In the past, it was fine for people to accomplish things deliberately over five or ten years. Today, the period in which results are evaluated has shortened to the point where even three years is too long of a wait. Things have reached such an extreme pace that even one year can be too long of a wait. People could be evaluated as a failure if they have not sprouted one year after taking a new position.

You must have higher abilities than the elite employees

These sorts of judgments are being made now, even in large companies. Even so, if you want to be independent and start your own business, you must be more excellent than the workers in your company who seem like they can be promoted. Otherwise, you will not be successful. If you do not have such abilities, you would be better off being hired at some company.

In the past, people said that less than one in five could succeed in starting a business. In an age of recession, this ratio has now become even smaller. If you would start a business, you must be able to take the risk, that is, only one in ten or one in twenty will be successful.

Therefore, it is an open question as to whether it is entirely good to start a new company. It is a fact that our society has now reached a high level of fluidity, so perhaps job changing has become more common than starting a business. "If someone with skills starts a company and that company fails, he can work somewhere else"—this idea will be the norm.

If you want to start your own business, you must be able to think and act more quickly than someone valued as an elite employee in a company. Only those who, while working in a company, find working at a slow pace very hard to bear are able to succeed. Those who only give enough ideas to be useful at their work in a department or section should not start their own business.

For example, suppose there is a person assigned to a department and thinks, "My section won't be able to use up my ideas, even if I remain here for 10 years. I'll take interest in the work of other departments. Moreover, I'll take interest in other industries." If you are this sort of person, you may well succeed at starting up a company. We could say we are in an age when people who used to be labeled as those who can't sit still are the ones with the opportunity.

In other words, people with the following are most apt to succeed in starting up a company.

First, people who have the ability to plan and give many ideas in various domains. These are people who do not simply dig one hole deep, but dig holes in various places. Such people are able to engage in so-called "lateral thinking" and put forth diverse ideas that are not related to each other.

Next, people who are apt to succeed are those who think and act much faster than an average employee.

Keeping in mind that since the success rate may be less than one in ten, you may want to find a job in another company if you fail. Failure to start a company surely means that you need someone with a higher level of management ability to show you the way.

Whether or not you have management ability can Only be found by practicing management

Management ability is, for the most part, an innate ability. A portion comes from the person's efforts, but the innate aspects form a large part of the ability. Management ability can only be found by practicing management, so this makes things difficult.

It is impossible to determine beforehand via school test whether someone has management ability. You will never know whether your company will survive, if you do not get the chance to act as the company president. There is no way of knowing whether you have management ability if you are not given the opportunity to practice it. It can be evaluated upon seeing the results, but you will not know unless you try.

This does not only apply to CEOs. Likewise, you will

not know the management abilities of the department heads or the section chiefs if they are not given the opportunity. The same goes for executives. In a large corporation, many of those appointed to executive positions are generally gone within two years or so. Apparently, even among those promoted from section chief to executive, 30 or 40 percent of them fail.

We see many cases of department heads that are good at their job, but fail in their ability once they become executives. Does this mean whoever put them in those positions made a mistake? Not necessarily. Until they are assigned to that position, there is no way of knowing whether they will succeed.

There may be quite a lot of people with roughly the same abilities, who are promoted from the department head positions to executive positions. Some of these people will succeed, while three or four in ten will fail. However, their promotion was not a mistake. It is only because you have appointed them to their positions that you can now see who are executive material and who are not. Some junior executives show more and more competence and become a managing director, senior managing director and finally the CEO. So, you will not know unless you put them in those positions.

Therefore, there is no test to measure the ability to start a venture company successfully. A person must actually do the job; only then can you see whether they will succeed or be weeded out.

Of course, sometimes people become adept through building "muscles" as they work hard at their new management positions. In general, however, management ability is largely an innate ability. For that reason, people without talent will fail, no matter how many times they manage a company.

Nonetheless, this is not something that you can see beforehand. Since you can only judge based on achievements, judgment will always come after the fact. Whether the judgment comes from a top scholar or an elite manager does not matter. Setting aside the question of how much time it takes to render a judgment, there is absolutely no way of knowing whether a person can be successful at starting a company unless he is given the chance. If you think you would be successful in starting a company, it is best to give it a try. If you try and fail, then there is nothing to do but change your occupation.

In Zen Buddhism, this is "to know cold and hot." You cannot determine whether water is cold or hot unless you put your hand in it. You will not know this, even if other people tell you so. If you put your hand in the water, you would understand whether it is lukewarm or hot. In the same way, you need to experience things firsthand in order to understand them.

In the case of starting a company, many uncertain factors lie that are impossible to forecast in advance. Management circumstances may change or products that were popular may lead to unexpected results. One of your products may become a hit, but the next one may not. You will face such type of risks.

Consulting people who know you very well

In addition to that, before starting a business, you should consult someone who knows you very well. It is good to have various discussions with people such as your family members, friends, and senior management colleagues.

Generally speaking, you will hear different opinions. If everyone agrees that you should not become a CEO, then perhaps your choice is a poor one.

Even if you listen to what people have to say, things may not turn out in such ways. In the end, you must take responsibility for your own, but it may be good to listen to various people as much as you think you need.

Usually, you can expect divided opinions. If everyone says you will succeed or if everyone says you will not succeed, then in both cases, there is probably something wrong. It is only natural for different opinions to exist, so it would be strange to get a very clear conclusion. It would be odd for a person who everyone says would certainly succeed in starting a new company to have been serving in a company for a long time. Suppose he works in a company. A person able to succeed at starting a business will have colleagues who have been saying for years that he could quit his job and become independent, that there is no need for him to stay with the company until retirement.

It is good to listen to opinions of the people around you, but in the end, you have to decide on your own.

The success rate today has dropped below one in ten. You can try to start your own business if you are dissatisfied with working in your current company. If you do so but find out that you lack management ability, you must go back to working under someone, even if it goes against your pride. It is better for you to realize that barely one in ten people possess management ability.

In order to determine whether you have the ability, you must try your hand at management.

Afterword

Be strict with yourself. Keep your guard up. Stop pointless spending. However, even with all this, companies do not survive. How are we to break out of the "Hatoyama-Ozawa Recession"* that will last for another 10 years? My mind is focused on this problem. A free economy within a socialist system is like a free enterprise in a prison—it is not free at all.

Yet, I will say this. Like a yacht moving forward against the wind, find a way to win by making use of your single business opportunity and build up a high value-added company. Though it may take time, people will eventually perceive their mistakes and realize who the true leader is.

You must give your best efforts and transform hardship into victory.

Ryuho Okawa
Founder and CEO of Happy Science Group
November 2009

---

* Yukio Hatoyama was the leader of Democratic Party of Japan, the political party that won by a landslide in the Japanese general elections held in August 2009. He became the prime minister in September 2009. Ichiro Ozawa was the DPJ leader before Hatoyama. Ozawa served as the secretary general during the Hatoyama administration.

ABOUT THE AUTHOR

Founder and CEO of Happy Science Group.

Ryuho Okawa was born on July 7th 1956, in Tokushima, Japan. After graduating from the University of Tokyo with a law degree, he joined a Tokyo-based trading house. While working at its New York headquarters, he studied international finance at the Graduate Center of the City University of New York. In 1981, he attained Great Enlightenment and became aware that he is El Cantare with a mission to bring salvation to all humankind.

In 1986, he established Happy Science. It now has members in over 165 countries across the world, with more than 700 branches and temples as well as 10,000 missionary houses around the world.

He has given over 3,450 lectures (of which more than 150 are in English) and published over 3,000 books (of which more than 600 are Spiritual Interview Series), and many are translated into 40 languages. Along with *The Laws of the Sun* and *The Laws Of Messiah*, many of the books have become best sellers or million sellers. To date, Happy Science has produced 25 movies. The original story and original concept were given by the Executive Producer Ryuho Okawa. He has also composed music and written lyrics of over 450 pieces.

Moreover, he is the Founder of Happy Science University and Happy Science Academy (Junior and Senior High School), Founder and President of the Happiness Realization Party, Founder and Honorary Headmaster of Happy Science Institute of Government and Management, Founder of IRH Press Co., Ltd., and the Chairperson of NEW STAR PRODUCTION Co., Ltd. and ARI Production Co., Ltd.

WHAT IS EL CANTARE?

El Cantare means "the Light of the Earth," and is the Supreme God of the Earth who has been guiding humankind since the beginning of Genesis. He is whom Jesus called Father and Muhammad called Allah, and is *Ame-no-Mioya-Gami*, Japanese Father God. Different parts of El Cantare's core consciousness have descended to Earth in the past, once as Alpha and another as Elohim. His branch spirits, such as Shakyamuni Buddha and Hermes, have descended to Earth many times and helped to flourish many civilizations. To unite various religions and to integrate various fields of study in order to build a new civilization on Earth, a part of the core consciousness has descended to Earth as Master Ryuho Okawa.

Alpha is a part of the core consciousness of El Cantare who descended to Earth around 330 million years ago. Alpha preached Earth's Truths to harmonize and unify Earth-born humans and space people who came from other planets.

Elohim is a part of El Cantare's core consciousness who descended to Earth around 150 million years ago. He gave wisdom, mainly on the differences of light and darkness, good and evil.

Ame-no-Mioya-Gami (Japanese Father God) is the Creator God and the Father God who appears in the ancient literature, *Hotsuma Tsutae*. It is believed that He descended on the foothills of Mt. Fuji about 30,000 years ago and built the Fuji dynasty, which is the root of the Japanese civilization. With justice as the central pillar, Ame-no-Mioya-Gami's teachings spread to ancient civilizations of other countries in the world.

Shakyamuni Buddha was born as a prince into the Shakya Clan in India around 2,600 years ago. When he was 29 years old, he renounced the world and sought enlightenment. He later attained Great Enlightenment and founded Buddhism.

Hermes is one of the 12 Olympian gods in Greek mythology, but the spiritual Truth is that he taught the teachings of love and progress around 4,300 years ago that became the origin of the current Western civilization. He is a hero that truly existed.

Ophealis was born in Greece around 6,500 years ago and was the leader who took an expedition to as far as Egypt. He is the God of miracles, prosperity, and arts, and is known as Osiris in the Egyptian mythology.

Rient Arl Croud was born as a king of the ancient Incan Empire around 7,000 years ago and taught about the mysteries of the mind. In the heavenly world, he is responsible for the interactions that take place between various planets.

Thoth was an almighty leader who built the golden age of the Atlantic civilization around 12,000 years ago. In the Egyptian mythology, he is known as god Thoth.

Ra Mu was a leader who built the golden age of the civilization of Mu around 17,000 years ago. As a religious leader and a politician, he ruled by uniting religion and politics.

ABOUT HAPPY SCIENCE

Happy Science is a global movement that empowers individuals to find purpose and spiritual happiness and to share that happiness with their families, societies, and the world. With more than 12 million members around the world, Happy Science aims to increase awareness of spiritual truths and expand our capacity for love, compassion, and joy so that together we can create the kind of world we all wish to live in.

Activities at Happy Science are based on the Principle of Happiness (Love, Wisdom, Self-Reflection, and Progress). This principle embraces worldwide philosophies and beliefs, transcending boundaries of culture and religions.

Love teaches us to give ourselves freely without expecting anything in return; it encompasses giving, nurturing, and forgiving.

Wisdom leads us to the insights of spiritual truths, and opens us to the true meaning of life and the will of God (the universe, the highest power, Buddha).

Self-Reflection brings a mindful, nonjudgmental lens to our thoughts and actions to help us find our truest selves—the essence of our souls—and deepen our connection to the highest power. It helps us attain a clean and peaceful mind and leads us to the right life path.

Progress emphasizes the positive, dynamic aspects of our spiritual growth—actions we can take to manifest and spread happiness around the world. It's a path that not only expands our soul growth, but also furthers the collective potential of the world we live in.

PROGRAMS AND EVENTS

The doors of Happy Science are open to all. We offer a variety of programs and events, including self-exploration and self-growth programs, spiritual seminars, meditation and contemplation sessions, study groups, and book events.

Our programs are designed to:
* Deepen your understanding of your purpose and meaning in life
* Improve your relationships and increase your capacity to love unconditionally
* Attain peace of mind, decrease anxiety and stress, and feel positive
* Gain deeper insights and a broader perspective on the world
* Learn how to overcome life's challenges
  ... and much more.

For more information, visit happy-science.org.

OUR ACTIVITIES

Happy Science does other various activities to provide support for those in need.

◆ **You Are An Angel! General Incorporated Association**
Happy Science has a volunteer network in Japan that encourages and supports children with disabilities as well as their parents and guardians.

◆ **Never Mind School for Truancy**
At 'Never Mind,' we support students who find it very challenging to attend schools in Japan. We also nurture their self-help spirit and power to rebound against obstacles in life based on Master Okawa's teachings and faith.

◆ **"Prevention Against Suicide" Campaign since 2003**
A nationwide campaign to reduce suicides; over 20,000 people commit suicide every year in Japan. "The Suicide Prevention Website-Words of Truth for You-" presents spiritual prescriptions for worries such as depression, lost love, extramarital affairs, bullying and work-related problems, thereby saving many lives.

◆ **Support for Anti-bullying Campaigns**
Happy Science provides support for a group of parents and guardians, Network to Protect Children from Bullying, a general incorporated foundation launched in Japan to end bullying, including those that can even be called a criminal offense. So far, the network received more than 5,000 cases and resolved 90% of them.

- **The Golden Age Scholarship**

  This scholarship is granted to students who can contribute greatly and bring a hopeful future to the world.

- **Success No.1**

  Buddha's Truth Afterschool Academy

  Happy Science has over 180 classrooms throughout Japan and in several cities around the world that focus on afterschool education for children. The education focuses on faith and morals in addition to supporting children's school studies.

- **Angel Plan V**

  For children under the age of kindergarten, Happy Science holds classes for nurturing healthy, positive, and creative boys and girls.

- **Future Stars Training Department**

  The Future Stars Training Department was founded within the Happy Science Media Division with the goal of nurturing talented individuals to become successful in the performing arts and entertainment industry.

- **NEW STAR PRODUCTION Co., Ltd.**

  ARI Production Co., Ltd.

  We have companies to nurture actors and actresses, artists, and vocalists. They are also involved in film production.

CONTACT INFORMATION

Happy Science is a worldwide organization with branches and temples around the globe. For a comprehensive list, visit the worldwide directory at *happy-science.org*. The following are some of the many Happy Science locations:

UNITED STATES AND CANADA

New York
79 Franklin St., New York, NY 10013, USA
Phone: 1-212-343-7972
Fax: 1-212-343-7973
Email: ny@happy-science.org
Website: happyscience-usa.org

New Jersey
66 Hudson St., #2R, Hoboken, NJ 07030, USA
Phone: 1-201-313-0127
Email: nj@happy-science.org
Website: happyscience-usa.org

Chicago
2300 Barrington Rd., Suite #400,
Hoffman Estates, IL 60169, USA
Phone: 1-630-937-3077
Email: chicago@happy-science.org
Website: happyscience-usa.org

Florida
5208 8th St., Zephyrhills, FL 33542, USA
Phone: 1-813-715-0000
Fax: 1-813-715-0010
Email: florida@happy-science.org
Website: happyscience-usa.org

Atlanta
1874 Piedmont Ave., NE Suite 360-C
Atlanta, GA 30324, USA
Phone: 1-404-892-7770
Email: atlanta@happy-science.org
Website: happyscience-usa.org

San Francisco
525 Clinton St.
Redwood City, CA 94062, USA
Phone & Fax: 1-650-363-2777
Email: sf@happy-science.org
Website: happyscience-usa.org

Los Angeles
1590 E. Del Mar Blvd., Pasadena, CA
91106, USA
Phone: 1-626-395-7775
Fax: 1-626-395-7776
Email: la@happy-science.org
Website: happyscience-usa.org

Orange County
16541 Gothard St. Suite 104
Huntington Beach, CA 92647
Phone: 1-714-659-1501
Email: oc@happy-science.org
Website: happyscience-usa.org

San Diego
7841 Balboa Ave. Suite #202
San Diego, CA 92111, USA
Phone: 1-626-395-7775
Fax: 1-626-395-7776
E-mail: sandiego@happy-science.org
Website: happyscience-usa.org

Hawaii
Phone: 1-808-591-9772
Fax: 1-808-591-9776
Email: hi@happy-science.org
Website: happyscience-usa.org

Kauai
3343 Kanakolu Street, Suite 5
Lihue, HI 96766, USA
Phone: 1-808-822-7007
Fax: 1-808-822-6007
Email: kauai-hi@happy-science.org
Website: happyscience-usa.org

Toronto

845 The Queensway
Etobicoke, ON M8Z 1N6, Canada
Phone: 1-416-901-3747
Email: toronto@happy-science.org
Website: happy-science.ca

Vancouver

#201-2607 East 49th Avenue,
Vancouver, BC, V5S 1J9, Canada
Phone: 1-604-437-7735
Fax: 1-604-437-7764
Email: vancouver@happy-science.org
Website: happy-science.ca

INTERNATIONAL

Tokyo

1-6-7 Togoshi, Shinagawa,
Tokyo, 142-0041, Japan
Phone: 81-3-6384-5770
Fax: 81-3-6384-5776
Email: tokyo@happy-science.org
Website: happy-science.org

Seoul

74, Sadang-ro 27-gil,
Dongjak-gu, Seoul, Korea
Phone: 82-2-3478-8777
Fax: 82-2-3478-9777
Email: korea@happy-science.org
Website: happyscience-korea.org

London

3 Margaret St.
London, W1W 8RE United Kingdom
Phone: 44-20-7323-9255
Fax: 44-20-7323-9344
Email: eu@happy-science.org
Website: www.happyscience-uk.org

Taipei

No. 89, Lane 155, Dunhua N. Road,
Songshan District, Taipei City 105, Taiwan
Phone: 886-2-2719-9377
Fax: 886-2-2719-5570
Email: taiwan@happy-science.org
Website: happyscience-tw.org

Sydney

516 Pacific Highway, Lane Cove North,
2066 NSW, Australia
Phone: 61-2-9411-2877
Fax: 61-2-9411-2822
Email: sydney@happy-science.org

Kuala Lumpur

No 22A, Block 2, Jalil Link Jalan Jalil
Jaya 2, Bukit Jalil 57000,
Kuala Lumpur, Malaysia
Phone: 60-3-8998-7877
Fax: 60-3-8998-7977
Email: malaysia@happy-science.org
Website: happyscience.org.my

Sao Paulo

Rua. Domingos de Morais 1154,
Vila Mariana, Sao Paulo SP
CEP 04010-100, Brazil
Phone: 55-11-5088-3800
Email: sp@happy-science.org
Website: happyscience.com.br

Kathmandu

Kathmandu Metropolitan City,
Ward No. 15, Ring Road, Kimdol,
Sitapaila Kathmandu, Nepal
Phone: 977-1-427-2931
Email: nepal@happy-science.org

Jundiai

Rua Congo, 447, Jd. Bonfiglioli
Jundiai-CEP, 13207-340, Brazil
Phone: 55-11-4587-5952
Email: jundiai@happy-science.org

Kampala

Plot 877 Rubaga Road, Kampala
P.O. Box 34130 Kampala, UGANDA
Phone: 256-79-4682-121
Email: uganda@happy-science.org

ABOUT HAPPINESS REALIZATION PARTY

The Happiness Realization Party (HRP) was founded in May 2009 by Master Ryuho Okawa as part of the Happy Science Group. HRP strives to improve the Japanese society, based on three basic political principles of "freedom, democracy, and faith," and let Japan promote individual and public happiness from Asia to the world as a leader nation.

1) Diplomacy and Security: Protecting Freedom, Democracy, and Faith of Japan and the World from China's Totalitarianism

Japan's current defense system is insufficient against China's expanding hegemony and the threat of North Korea's nuclear missiles. Japan, as the leader of Asia, must strengthen its defense power and promote strategic diplomacy together with the nations which share the values of freedom, democracy, and faith. Further, HRP aims to realize world peace under the leadership of Japan, the nation with the spirit of religious tolerance.

2) Economy: Early economic recovery through utilizing the "wisdom of the private sector"

Economy has been damaged severely by the novel coronavirus originated in China. Many companies have been forced into bankruptcy or out of business. What is needed for economic recovery now is not subsidies and regulations by the government, but policies which can utilize the "wisdom of the private sector."

For more information, visit en.hr-party.jp

HAPPY SCIENCE ACADEMY JUNIOR AND SENIOR HIGH SCHOOL

Happy Science Academy Junior and Senior High School is a boarding school founded with the goal of educating the future leaders of the world who can have a big vision, persevere, and take on new challenges.

Currently, there are two campuses in Japan; the Nasu Main Campus in Tochigi Prefecture, founded in 2010, and the Kansai Campus in Shiga Prefecture, founded in 2013.

Nasu Main Campus

Kansai Campus

ABOUT HS PRESS

HS Press is an imprint of IRH Press Co., Ltd. IRH Press Co., Ltd., based in Tokyo, was founded in 1987 as a publishing division of Happy Science. IRH Press publishes religious and spiritual books, journals, magazines and also operates broadcast and film production enterprises. For more information, visit *okawabooks.com*.

Follow us on:

- Facebook: Okawa Books
- Youtube: Okawa Books
- Pinterest: Okawa Books
- Instagram: OkawaBooks
- Twitter: Okawa Books
- Goodreads: Ryuho Okawa

NEWSLETTER

To receive book related news, promotions and events, please subscribe to our newsletter below.

eepurl.com/bsMeJj

AUDIO / VISUAL MEDIA

YOUTUBE

PODCAST

Introduction of Ryuho Okawa's titles; topics ranging from self-help, current affairs, spirituality, religion, and the universe.

BOOKS BY RYUHO OKAWA

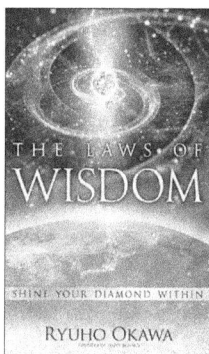

THE LAWS OF WISDOM
SHINE YOUR DIAMOND WITHIN

This book guides you along the path on how to acquire wisdom, so that you can break through any wall you will confront in your life or in your business. By reading this book, you will be able to avoid getting lost in the flood of information and, going beyond the level of just amassing knowledge, be able to come up with many great ideas, make effective planning and strategy and develop your leadership while receiving good inspiration.

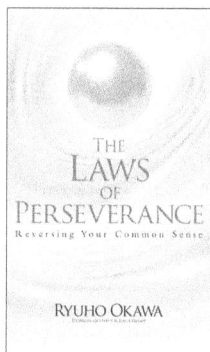

THE LAWS OF PERSEVERANCE
REVERSING YOUR COMMON SENSE

"No matter how much you suffer, the Truth will gradually shine forth as you continue to endure hardships. Therefore, simply strengthen your mind and keep making constant efforts in times of endurance, however ordinary they may be. "

-From Postscript

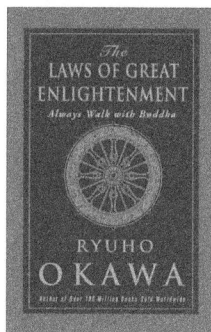

THE LAWS OF GREAT ENLIGHTENMENT
ALWAYS WALK WITH BUDDHA

In this modern society, we often find ourselves unable to forgive someone and maintain a peaceful mind. However, there are ways to lead a stress-free life and enjoy happiness from within. This book offers the practical approaches to achieve it. By understanding the Buddhist concept of "enlightenment," you will gain the power to forgive sins and get to know how to be the master of your own mind.

For a complete list of books, visit okawabooks.com

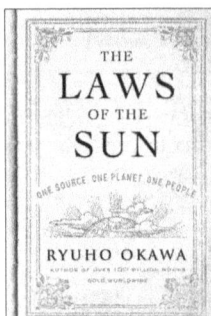

THE LAWS OF THE SUN
ONE SOURCE, ONE PLANET, ONE PEOPLE

IMAGINE IF YOU COULD ASK GOD why He created this world and what spiritual laws He used to shape us—and everything around us. If we could understand His designs and intentions, we could discover what our goals in life should be and whether our actions move us closer to those goals or farther away.

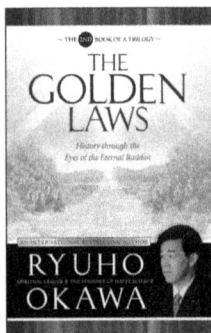

THE GOLDEN LAWS
HISTORY THROUGH THE EYES OF THE ETERNAL BUDDHA

The Golden Laws reveals how Buddha's Plan has been unfolding on earth, and outlines five thousand years of the secret history of humankind. Once we understand the true course of history, we cannot help but become aware of the significance of our spiritual mission in the present age.

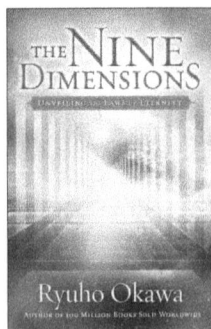

THE NINE DIMENSIONS
UNVEILING THE LAWS OF ETERNITY

This book is a window into the mind of our loving God, who encourages us to grow into greater angels. It reveals His deepest intentions, answering the timely question of why He conceived such a colorful medley of religions, philosophies, sciences, arts, and other forms of expression.

For a complete list of books, visit okawabooks.com

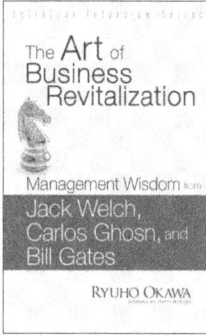

THE ART OF BUSINESS REVITALIZATION

MANAGEMENT WISDOM FROM JACK WELCH, CARLOS GHOSN, AND BILL GATES

In this book, Master Ryuho Okawa conducts spiritual interviews with three of the greatest executives of our time. General Electric's Jack Welch, Renault and Nissan's Carlos Ghosn, and Microsoft's Bill Gates give readers a glimpse into how they took hold of opportunities and turned them into successes.

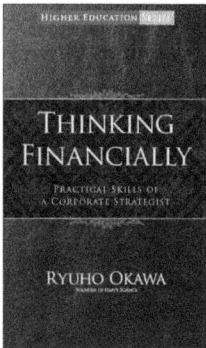

THINKING FINANCIALLY
PRACTICAL SKILLS OF A CORPORATE STRATEGIST

"As the founder of Happy Science, I attained both spiritual and philosophical enlightenment. Not only that, but my background in international business development and as a management professional – a financial expert at a trading company – have been a great driving force in the progress of this religion."

-From Afterword

For a complete list of books, visit okawabooks.com

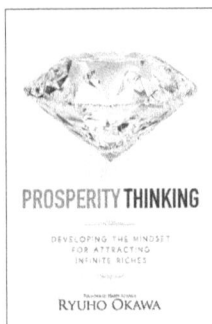

PROSPERITY THINKING
DEVELOPING THE MINDSET FOR ATTRACTING INFINITE RICHES

When you think about wealth, its starting point is to benefit more and more people. Or, put differently, being wealthy is to be appreciated by more and more people. This is the source of wealth.

-From Chapter 2

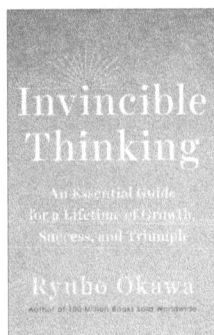

INVINCIBLE THINKING
AN ESSENTIAL GUIDE FOR A LIFETIME OF GROWTH, SUCCESS, AND TRIUMPH

In this book, Ryuho Okawa lays out the principles of invincible thinking that will allow us to achieve long-lasting triumph. This powerful and unique philosophy is not only about becoming successful or achieving our goal in life, but also about building the foundation of life that becomes the basis of our life-long, lasting success and happiness.

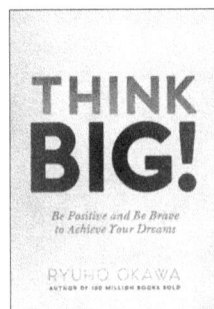

THINK BIG!
BE POSITIVE AND BE BRAVE TO ACHIEVE YOUR DREAMS!

"Every individual faces unique problems and circumstances, and what is most important is that no matter what we are faced with, we continue to dream big. We received the gift of life, so we might as well think big and live life to its full potential."

-From Chapter 3

For a complete list of books, visit okawabooks.com